THE GOOD FAT DIET

THE GOOD FAT DIET

*Robert Gold, M.D.,
and Kerry Rose-Gold*

BANTAM BOOKS
TORONTO · NEW YORK · LONDON · SYDNEY · AUCKLAND

Caution: **Fitness, diet and health are matters which necessarily vary from individual to individual. We recommend that you speak with your doctor about your individual needs before starting this or any other diet program. Consulting your physician is especially important if you are on any medication or are already under medical care for any illness (especially bleeding disorders). If you have known fish allergies you are advised not to attempt this program.**

THE GOOD FAT DIET
A Bantam Book / February 1987

Library of Congress Cataloging-in-Publication Data

Gold, Robert, 1952–
  The good fat diet.

  Bibliography: p. 175
  Includes index.
  1. Low-cholesterol diet.   2. Reducing diets.
3. Complex carbohydrate diet.   4. Low-cholesterol diet—
Recipes.   5. Reducing diets—Recipes.   6. Complex
carbohydrate diet—Recipes.   7. Cookery (Fish)   I. Rose-
Gold, Kerry, 1953–   . II. Title.
RM237.75.G65   1987   613.2'8   86-26583
ISBN 0-553-05186-5

Published simultaneously in the United States and Canada

Bantam Books are published by Bantam Books, Inc. Its trademark, consisting of the words "Bantam Books" and the portrayal of a rooster, is Registered in U.S. Patent and Trademark Office and in other countries. Marca Registrada. Bantam Books, Inc., 666 Fifth Avenue, New York, New York 10103.

*In pursuit of good health
through better nutrition*

We would like to extend our thanks to our friends, our parents: Marilyn and Lou Perlin, Gertrude and David Gold, Ann Newman, and our families, and special thanks to: Ken Rose, whose constant attention and concern made our work easier; Steven Chain and Elizabeth Fox, whose care of the manuscript was invaluable; Jim and Elizabeth Trupin, who breathed life into our idea; and finally to Coleen O'Shea, who realized the importance of publishing this kind of book.

Contents

1.

It's Modern and It Works!

"How can you eat all that?"

"You eat everything?"

"How can you eat so much and not get fat?"

My friends and family are surprised how easily I maintain my 5'2", 110-pound figure, even after giving birth to our daughter. They've seen my husband, Bob, quickly grow slimmer by twenty pounds while lowering a dangerously elevated cholesterol level. They know that Bob is a doctor. They're also aware that we've been developing a weight-loss breakthrough, which we call The Good Fat Diet. They're excited to hear how our experience may relate to them.

A lot of my friends, like most of us, have been on and off all sorts of diets. But today they're mostly concerned with two things. They want to keep their shapes youthful and protect their health against the deteriorating effects of aging. And, of course, they're interested in a program that helps them lose weight fast! And so when I tell them that on The Good Fat Diet it's easy to lose as much as ten pounds in two weeks, that with this program they can keep their figures in line while protecting their hearts against disease, it's no wonder they're curious to know the secrets of our revolutionary rapid-weight-loss plan.

"Imagine," I say, "the worst things we've been told that you can eat—a diet loaded with fat and cholesterol, and hardly any fiber, complex carbohydrates, or vitamins like C or E. You would suspect that anyone eating this unbalanced diet would not be long among the living. Yet, at a remote village in western Greenland the Eskimos eat exactly this type of diet—and they're healthier than the average American."

"How can this high-fat diet be healthy?" my friends ask in disbelief.

"Along with all the other fats and cholesterols," I explain, "their diet also contains what is known as a *good fat.*"

Scientists call this good fat, which is found in certain foods, *Omega-3.* They believe the effect of *Omega-3* on normal body metabolism helps protect the Eskimos from disease states caused by excess dietary fats and cholesterol. Scientists who studied these Eskimos noted among them an astonishingly low incidence of heart attacks, hardened arteries, and high blood pressure. They found that their blood actually contained less cholesterol than the typical American's: diabetes was unknown, arthritis and hypertension were uncommon. In effect, the good fat neutralized the dangers of their high-fat diet. This discovery can have an enormous impact on our diet.

I tell my friends that The Good Fat Diet will help them lose weight fast in a simple, practical, healthy way. They can get the added benefit of weight loss and reduce the risk of heart disease if they: *"Eat less red meat. Eat fish two or three times a week, alternating with chicken."*

Red meat is high in "bad fat." The bad fat leads to obesity. Red meat contains too much of the "saturated" variety of fats compared to the "unsaturated" good fats found in fish. Saturated fats are also present in nutritionally harmful amounts in dairy products, certain vegetable oils, such as coconut oil, and in eggs. Fish has fewer calories and we know that eating fish is "slimming." But fish, especially certain varieties of fish, along with other marine animals, contain the *Omega-3 good fat.* What the amazing findings of the latest Eskimo-diet research studies proved was that certain fish especially rich in *Omega-3* not only can be used in a diet program to help shed pounds quickly, but also appear to be uniquely beneficial to preventing and perhaps even reversing the damage of America's leading killer—heart disease.

The Good Fat Diet is different from other diets that promote rapid weight loss. Like Scarsdale, one of the most successful quick-reducing programs of the past, The Good Fat Diet takes off ten pounds in just two weeks. But unlike most other popular rapid-weight-loss plans, our program obtains this result without adding an increased burden to the heart.

In The Good Fat Diet, seafood is both diet food *and* health food.

It's diet food because, being "calorie efficient," it produces rapid weight loss. It's health food because the workings of *Omega-3* have been shown to effectively and efficiently combat heart disease.

The Good Fat Diet is a special fish-based rapid-weight-loss plan. It's in line with the latest in biomedical thinking. It has elements in common with the food eaten by our ancestors the cavemen, as well as by today's Eskimos, whose greatly reduced heart disease rate, scientists now believe, is due to their high intake of the good fat contained in fish.

2.

Escape from the Land of the "Red-Meat Eaters"

Bob and I are in our early thirties. Bob is an internist with a busy schedule. Though lately I've been working out of the house and taking care of our small baby, I am a biochemist.

The rapid-weight-loss program rich in *Omega-3* that my husband and I created had its origin in a mixture of motives. On the one hand, we were weight conscious. In my case, I wished to maintain my petite figure. My husband was overweight and wanted to lose twenty pounds rapidly. At the same time we were worried about a history of heart disease in both our families. When we learned about *Omega-3* and developed The Good Fat Diet, we came up with the diet solution that provided the perfect answer to all our major health concerns.

Until then our diet had been typical of most Americans of our generation. Raised in the affluent postwar years on a high-protein, high-fat diet—the "red meat-and-potato" mentality—we became accustomed to an eating routine that later played havoc with our health and weight. Before The Good Fat Diet, when Bob was just beginning his medical career, he was a consistent violator of the principles of good nutrition, which he had studied at U.C.L.A. medical school. Defying his own better sense, he would hurriedly grab a couple of greasy hamburgers, a soda, or a submarine sandwich on the run between appointments. Bob was like many people who believe that they will never be one of the statistics. Even doctors are not immune to thinking, "Bad things only happen to others." But the reality soon became clear. After a year of marriage, Bob had gained twenty pounds and had established an eating pattern that could have led to serious medical problems.

Cooking has always been fun for both of us. We loved red meat and eggs and dairy products and mayonnaise and everything else that raises cholesterol levels. This type of diet with its nutritional deficiencies encouraged Bob's weight gain. Within one year his pants size had increased twice, and at thirty-two he was developing a double chin.

Then one day we realized we were facing real medical problems; problems that could be life threatening.

"IF YOU DON'T HELP ME, I'M DEAD MEAT!"

Shortly after our first anniversary my husband returned from the bedside of his mother, who that afternoon had suffered a heart attack. While sitting with her, it had suddenly occurred to him that her entire side of the family had died of heart attacks while in their fifties. His father, too, had already sustained two heart attacks.

"My whole family is dying of this," Bob said. "I'm the perfect candidate for a bypass." He added wryly, "I'd better drop some pounds fast. If you don't help me, I'm dead meat!"

Now the project he had dillydallied with for months—namely, to lose twenty pounds—couldn't be ignored any longer. The diet he needed was not merely one that would help him regain the body of his youth. But as a doctor, Bob knew that being overweight constituted the outward sign of a more deadly process within, where arteries' walls "put on weight" in the form of cholesterol, ultimately blocking the flow of blood to the heart.

As for myself, though I did not require the rapid weight reduction Bob needed, I had not escaped the battle against the bulge. Yet, for the first time in my life I experienced the problem of maintaining the weight I had been able to keep without effort since I was nineteen.

We realized the need for a diet that would not just take off weight or maintain it at the desired level. A really effective diet had to be both wholesome and delicious, as well as beneficial to the heart.

Bob and I talked it over and agreed that we had to put away a lot of the things we normally ate. We *had* to become as scientific about our way of losing weight and keeping it off as we were about other things in our life. Since I was doing most of the cooking, from a practical point of view it was up to me to come up with our new eating program. I soon discovered that our conventional fat-rich foods, particularly red meat, did not fit into this envisioned diet. Fish, with the good *Omega-3* fat, did—and in more ways than one, as I happily found out.

THE DIET OF THE FUTURE

With my training as a biochemist, I conducted the study and research for The Good Fat Diet jointly with my husband, who contributed his medical knowledge. We set out to take a radical departure from the typical weight-loss programs. We were looking for the diet of the future.

We wanted a diet like Scarsdale or Atkins, but without the bad fats such diets with their emphasis on red-meat-based protein contain. At last we succeeded in creating a weight-loss-effective and healthful alternative that put an end to the rule of bad fat, red meat, and other dietary "killers," such as cholesterol, triglycerides, calories, sugars, and empty carbohydrates.

The diet based on the *Omega-3*–bearing fish, with their astonishing effect on the arteries and heart disease, enabled Bob to achieve his rapid weight loss and weight control without sacrificing his health. At the same time I discovered that this fish-centered eating plan was a dieter's dream in one other very important way as well.

The Good Fat Diet made the goal of rapid weight loss achievable by eliminating toil and trouble in the kitchen. It fitted into our lifestyle. In fact, I would say that of all foods, fish is best suited to the modern woman, who often balances motherhood and a career.

When I first explained the principles of The Good Fat Diet to my friends, they reacted according to the time-worn notions held by many of our generation who believe that a meal without red meat must be boring, difficult to prepare, or both. I combated these errors with all my newfound knowledge and experience of creating fish-centered menus. I told them of the incredible weight-loss success I had observed in my own family. I informed them that far from struggling long hours with preparation and recipes, The Good Fat Diet let me spend more time with my family.

By formulating The Good Fat Diet, I found fish is not only wonderfully healthful and slimming, but contrary to what people think, it is a most exciting food component that needs no further testimony than that it is eaten the world over in an infinite variety of cooking traditions. The fish that promotes rapid weight loss and cuts down heart disease risk, unlike most other foods, can be eaten regularly without ever becoming humdrum. Only a few fundamental principles are required for its preparation. There are hundreds of delicious fish recipes and techniques that anyone can master instantly, as this book will show.

Another important point that had to be answered in my diet concerned "appetite satisfaction." No diet would suit my family unless it met the overriding criteria of being both tasty and filling. In order to stick to our healthy and balanced diet over the long term, it had to appeal to the palate and leave the feeling of having eaten something substantial. Because The Good Fat Diet provides fat in a beneficial form—a form, moreover, that makes weight loss sure and speedy—it satisfies the body's natural craving for fat, which in turn helps the slimming process by keeping the stomach contented.

CLEANER ARTERIES, GREATER LONGEVITY

Fish was first incorporated into our weekly menu plan as the basis of a rapid-weight-loss program designed for my husband. From there it was extended to maintain both my own and Bob's weight at the desired level. It also served to implant sound nutritional habits in ourselves and our daughter.

But more than just looking trim and slim, it was good to know that The Good Fat Diet helped remove fat from the outside as well as from within, where cleaner arteries mean greater longevity.

My own quest for weight loss and health had begun at home, where The Good Fat Diet was first put into practice. Here I first observed its incredible effectiveness. Bob's extra twenty pounds vanished quickly. We both felt lighter, more energetic. And like all new converts we wished to communicate our findings.

We wished to share our new dietary knowledge with all who still wandered, as we once had, among the tribes of nutritionally backward "red-meat eaters." We felt we had made a breakthrough. One thing I knew for certain: All new diets of the future would have to incorporate the principles and features of The Good Fat Diet.

3.

Good Fat in the American Kitchen

Most of our contemporaries belong to a generation that is more health and weight conscious than that of our parents, who probably did not count calories and very likely accepted body weight as an uncontrollable affair.

We've been more fortunate. As the beneficiaries of a greater nutritional awareness, we've grown used to hearing fat-rich foods condemned by such institutions as the National Cancer Institute and the American Heart Association. Many of us may be familiar with the recommendations made by the McGovern Committee and the National Academy of Sciences involving a "rebalancing" of the American diet through a drastic reduction of fat intake. We have all probably seen or heard the statistic that half the deaths in this country are caused by atherosclerosis, the process which clogs up the arteries to the heart with deposits of cholesterol and fat.

Having discovered the method of replacing this bad fat with good fat, we were able to form a diet that shed excess pounds in a manner both quick and in line with the latest medical findings. But even more important, with The Good Fat Diet we were also able to do something about heart disease, in particular its most common arteriosclerotic form, which has been associated with cholesterol.

OMEGA-3 AND CHOLESTEROL

In the early stage of my research, the dietary knowledge of greatest importance dealt with the subject of cholesterol. As I advanced deeper into the issues of weight loss, particularly as it related to the prevention of heart disease, I came to a fascinating understanding of the role of fish and its effect on dietary cholesterol. This came about through my research into recent scientific discoveries of the astounding effects of *Omega-3*, the good fat contained in many varieties of fish, and its function in preventing the scourge of heart disease.

Just as there is a good fat and bad fat, I learned there is a "good cholesterol" and "bad cholesterol." This biomedical fact explains how a person could be thin on the outside and "fat" on the inside, that is, having arteries with cholesterol-caked walls, which could lead to heart disease and death.

Thus, the first action I took was probably not unlike that which many of my contemporaries in a similar situation might have taken. All dangerous and "fattening" substances known to be high in cholesterol were banned from my kitchen. Red meat, along with mayonnaise, eggs, dairy products, was ruled from the fridge. Salt and sugar were severely restricted. The recipes for beef Wellington and fettuccine Alfredo were put away. Oils, butter, and margarine became ingredients that were used in limited amounts. And in the same flurry of dietary housecleaning I began to use more grains, especially rice, with our meals.

Chicken, veal, and fish naturally recommended themselves as the most suitable replacements for red meat on a low-calorie, rapid-weight-reduction program. With these "lean meats," which were at the same time valuable sources of protein, I possessed the basics of The Good Fat Diet. I was beginning to cut down our family's main source of cholesterol intake by a considerable percentage.

After his mother's heart attack Bob took a blood test that revealed cholesterol levels that ominously ranged toward the "elevated" side. It reminded him of the fact that for him losing weight was not merely a matter of "getting in shape for summer." It made him realize that his being moderately overweight was a symptom of a serious cholesterol-related disease syndrome in his family.

Later in the year, after The Good Fat Diet had become part of our eating routine, it was a moment of triumph when Bob announced a surprising drop in his serum cholesterol levels.

It proved the good fat, *Omega-3*, was working.

A COMPLETE AND BALANCED WAY OF EATING

Many of my husband's patients suffer from the modern scourges— cancer, heart disease, obesity, diabetes, rheumatoid arthritis. Precisely how far their diets, with the abundance of cholesterol, sugars, and fats, had contributed to their disease states would be difficult to say, but that there was an incontrovertible link pointed to by *every* medical authority was enough to convince me that we were killing ourselves by the food we consumed. To my husband and me it meant that a dietary program with the single aim of rapid weight loss would always fall short of the desired object, which was to change the way we eat to improve our overall health and well-being.

In this respect, of the countless diet plans I examined, studying the recipes and even their chemical composition, there was not one that satisfied me. Many of them were eminently sound in terms of nutritional balance, but they fell short of the guidelines I had established for our diet program for total health.

The closest I got to finding a program that came anywhere near the object of my search was *The McDougall Plan*. If the weight loss was not altogether rapid it was at least safe.

Its authors were young medical professionals applying science in the service of combating obesity and ill health. Dr. John McDougall struck a responsive chord in me because it seemed that he had once been very much like Bob, describing himself as a "reformed American eater who gorged on hamburger, french fries and ice cream." At one time Dr. McDougall had carried fifty pounds' overweight, which he subsequently lost by following his own "starch-based" diet that allowed him, he claimed, to "eat more and weigh less."

Although I admired McDougall's thoroughness on nutrition, dealing as he did with the same issues that interested Bob and me, it was obvious to me that his diet was impractical. It constituted too much of a departure from the normal eating style. It was also too *fat* stringent.

McDougall was asking that I perform culinary acrobatics with obscure spices and complicated substitutes, such as using coconut milk to give food a cheesy taste, and many other inventive substitutions to simulate different flavors. His approach was basically vegetarian and that in a manner so scientific that it bordered on the clinical. McDougall considered the rare fish or piece of chicken (no more than once a year!) a "feast food."

Such an austere regimen could never suit me or my family. It was bound to lead Bob back to the forbidden land of the "red-meat eaters." It was sure to make hash out of his efforts to lose weight because the McDougall plan was simply too strict.

THE BOTTOM LINE

Virtually all the other diets worthy of attention fell in the uninspired "1200-calories-a-day" range. Such diets were harmless and did what they promised to do regarding weight loss. I objected not to their nutritional integrity, but to the fact that they could only serve temporary weight-reducing goals.

They were the familiar diet refrain: low fat, high fiber, complex carbohydrates, lean meats. Countless dieters have gone on and off programs of this ilk. These programs complicate rather than alleviate the dieter's chief nemesis: the up-and-down, weight-loss/weight-gain swing of the pendulum, which is both unsatisfactory and unhealthy.

As a doctor, Bob agreed that the bottom line was *permanent* weight loss and *continued* good health. He said how pleased he should be to be able to offer his patients a plan that could deliver these results. And so with an after-dinner glass of *white* wine (fewer calories!), we renewed the pact that eventually became the revolutionary weight-loss program called The Good Fat Diet—a complete diet program that serves up fish dishes several times a week that are enjoyable, varied, delicious, wholesome, and "slimming."

4.

Not All Fats Are Evil

Early on in our project Bob had told me, "If we're going to eat fish, you will have to help me get to like it."

Bob had the red-meat eater's suspicion of the scaly species. Fish was suspect for being too ... "fishy."

Yet, everyone who has ever followed a weight-loss program knows that fish is low in calories. Doctors value it for its "nutrient density." Fish is packed with protein, vitamins, minerals, and oils crucial to our bodies. And now when it appeared that *Omega-3* might be an important preventive element against heart disease, Bob began to look at fish differently.

I first learned about *Omega-3* when Bob brought home from his clinic the bible of conservative medical thinking, the *New England Journal of Medicine*. In the May 9, 1985, issue, I read for the first time about the Eskimos who ate virtually nothing but "cholesterol blubber," yet who were paradoxically among the healthiest people in the world, practically free from heart disease and obesity. Incredibly, the prestigious *Journal* seemed to suggest that not all animal fats were evil!

The fatty cold-water fish eaten by the Eskimos appeared to be responsible for their remarkable health and fitness. This food source apparently helped keep blood pressure down, and the Eskimos' blood was found to be "thinner" and thus less susceptible to the blood clots that trigger heart attacks. The revolutionary good fat called *Omega-3*, which is contained in fish, according to the newly published report, also seemed to be effective against certain skin disorders, such as eczema and psoriasis, as well as against inflammatory conditions, such as arthritis. The good fat was even said to help brain development.

According to the *New England Journal of Medicine,* as little as one or two fish dishes per week might be of preventive value in combating coronary heart disease. It cited a Dutch study that found that people who ate as little as one ounce of fish per day had a 50 percent lower mortality rate from heart disease than those who did not eat fish—due to the fact, scientists said, that fish fats *lower* cholesterol levels.

The name they gave this good fat sounds like something out of science fiction, but *Omega-3* refers to the chemical formula whereby a class of fatty acids formed their first unsaturated bond between the third and fourth carbon. According to the *Journal, Omega-3* appeared to be involved in the remarkable cholesterol-reducing metabolism of the Eskimos. *Omega-3* seemed to be something in the nature of a "natural antifreeze," a type of fat that did not harden even at extremely low temperatures, helping keep fish metabolism fluid even in the cold North Atlantic and Pacific waters.

Medical statistics proclaim heart disease as the cause of death for over 50 percent of all Americans. This gruesome figure is often blamed on the average American diet with its dangerously high content of serum cholesterol (the level of cholesterol in the blood). For years now, the medical establishment has routinely issued warnings that the wrong diet can cause a heart attack because it can lead to higher concentrations of serum cholesterol, increasing the risk of coronary disease. Now studies have shown that reducing serum cholesterol can slow the progression of preexisting coronary disease. A change in diet is the usual first step to effect reductions of cholesterol. That's why we believed the discovery of *Omega-3* to be a significant breakthrough. It meant that though other dietary means might reduce cholesterol by a small percentage at best, now it seemed that by following a fish-centered diet rich in *Omega-3* we can lower cholesterol by a far more significant percentage!

"FISH REVOLUTION"

No sooner had my diet plan crystallized in the good fat formula than I made a surprising discovery. Unwittingly my choice had led me to join a trend that appeared to have been under steam for some time. People were already eating far more fish than ever before. Only to confirmed red-meat eaters like ourselves could this reality have been obscured for so long.

Fish markets were to be found in every neighborhood. Suddenly there was an astonishing variety of fish restaurants from which to choose, and fishmongers were happily complying with the demand by introducing more and more new species into the market. And if the crowds at the supermarket fish counters and the long waits at seafood restaurants needed further corroboration, the statistics gave additional proof that a shift in the eating spectrum was taking place. Last year almost 50 percent of consumers were serving more seafood than they did two years earlier, according to studies made by the West Coast Fisheries, and in the total volume of food served, restaurants reported that fish topped red meat and poultry.

Bob had been raised on red meat and potatoes, and the habits of a lifetime had left him lacking in the connoisseurship of fish. I wanted Bob to be able to easily distinguish sole from tuna or trout from sea bass: I wanted him to ask for red snapper as enthusiastically as he formerly did for T-Bone. Therefore, my first task was to introduce him to the species, varieties, tastes, and uses of fish, fresh as well as frozen. Fish high in fat, such as tuna and salmon, were as good as, if not better than, from the cholesterol standpoint, fish low in fat, such as cod and flounder, according to the latest scientific evidence.

I discovered that the finned creatures of our own North Atlantic and Pacific were particularly rich in *Omega-3*. Although these healthful fatty acids were found to some extent in all seafood, they are most abundant in cold-water fish, including rainbow trout, sardines, blue-fish, whitefish, and eel. So I cast my net wide, bringing to our table salmon, haddock, herring, mackerel, and red snapper, baked, broiled, or poached in dozens of delicious ways.

In shopping for ingredients and selecting fish, I found that behind the supermarket meat counters the attendants suddenly seemed to have become surprisingly knowledgeable about fish. I received helpful tips that have proved of lasting value in preparing our newfound bounty from the sea. In other fish markets I learned what bones to select for the fish stock that is the basis of many good fish recipes.

I also discovered easy and fascinating techniques to create delicious fish-rice-and-vegetable combinations, which can be practiced by anyone. Such dishes ensured that The Good Fat Diet would never become tiresome.

"YOU CAN EVEN MAKE FISH TASTE LIKE STEAK!"

I had chosen the good *Omega-3* fat as the nucleus of my rapid-weight-loss diet first of all for reasons of health and nutrition. But I was now to be initiated into the easy, practical, and delicious experience of fish cookery. The endless variety of exciting dishes that can be conjured from fish, rice, vegetables, and other low-calorie items was perhaps the most surprising discovery of all.

When I assembled the recipes and put together The Good Fat Diet, I ruled out the more exotic and rare varieties of fish. I eliminated complex dishes, and I decided that for each fish dish I created I must go to the place of origin, where it had been longest cultivated as a food.

One of my great discoveries, however, was the quality and abundant variety of fish dishes offered in our own country. Fish eating thrives in American regional cooking; the South, for instance, offers in Cajun cooking many wonderful fish recipes in combination with vegetables and rice.

Regional American, French, Italian, Caribbean, Chinese, British, Spanish, indeed, I discovered that every way of cooking fish known to man is represented in Los Angeles, our hometown. From all of them I learned and created. I knew I had succeeded when one day Bob paid me what I consider a stunning compliment.

"Kerry," he announced, "I don't miss meat. You are amazing! You can even make fish taste like steak!"

5.

How the Wrong Diet Can Prevent Rapid Weight Loss

Bob in his professional practice and I in my social circle have met all sorts of dieters, including the "kooky" ones who suck a grapefruit for breakfast, lunch, and dinner, or those who champion kelp extract, and even those who try to "wash away" obesity by subsisting largely on water. Most of my friends were devoted calorie counters.

But by far we found the average dieter to be a sensible person who is convinced that he is following a proven program. This same sensible person, however, usually gets insensibly frustrated over the reappearance of pounds that had been believed lost forever.

Bob has studied the up-and-down woes resulting from these diets. The "roller coaster effect," as it is called, became an all too familiar experience to many followers of the popular diets that came upon us in the seventies. Their advocacy of a high-protein/low-carbohydrate food plan turned out, upon closer examination, to be better described as a high-fat/high-cholesterol diet. The "roller coaster effect" that these diets gave rise to could only be expected from programs that ignored the fact that sound nutrition is inseparable from permanent weight loss and health.

Many people are under the mistaken belief that when they lose weight some of the 30–40 billion fat cells that are in the body of the average adult have disappeared. Medical opinion, however, holds that fat cells, just like brain cells, being vital to life function, do not disappear. They may shrink in size but become "fat" again as food becomes available. In fact, it is thought that during the weight gain *after* weight loss a considerable amount of extra fat and cholesterol is laid down in the arteries. This may be another result of the "roller coaster effect."

By the light of the latest medical and biochemical understanding of how fat forms, we were led to the inevitable conclusion that the high-protein diets like Scarsdale and Atkins are both ineffective and nutritionally unsound. Since its net effect may be to deposit *more* fats in the body and in the arteries, at best this type of diet merely redistributes the fat—from outside to inside the body. In so doing, an additional burden is placed on the heart, contributing to long-term cardiovascular failure and other disease states.

Besides the obvious stress this type of diet places on heart function, it also has a disruptive effect on homeostasis, the body's balance. Moreover, followers of this type of diet soon discover that their weight loss is really a water loss, since the high-protein diets work on the principle of ketosis, in which poorly burned fatty acids—ketones— stimulate urinary losses. This partly explains the "roller coaster effect," for little or no fat is lost. The body merely experiences a temporary water loss that usually occurs within the diet's initial eight- to ten-day period.

WEIGHT LOSS VERSUS FAT LOSS

A greater health consciousness appears to have arrived with the onset of the current decade. The new concern for health in the eighties is reflected by diets that have abandoned the "magic bullet" approach to slimming. They appear to have absorbed the scientific research pinpointing the difference between weight loss and fat loss. Besides being the chief reason why people gain weight, fat is now recognized in nutritionist and medical circles as implicated in the most deadly of the modern plagues—heart disease.

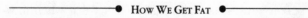

● HOW WE GET FAT ●

Fat is the most compact package of calories—and energy— the body stores. It's because this source of energy is so dense and concentrated that it takes a long time to burn. This is why many people find it difficult to lose weight: Once the diet is started the body resists by burning the calories at an even lower rate.

Fat can be made from any food component, i.e., carbohydrates, proteins, or fats. These are broken down in the stomach by enzymes, resulting in amino acids and glucose as well as minute fat droplets, which, after being processed in the liver, enter the bloodstream to supply energy to vital organs.

What the body does not use up is stored in fat cells for release when more energy is required. The fat cells consist of a nucleus that never disappears, regardless of the shrinking of the fat cell itself. "Putting on weight" means the fat cells around the nucleus are swelling by absorbing greater amounts of fat from food components.

The new breed of nutritionists advocates a return to safe and balanced dieting and addresses the role of fat in weight-loss programs that are generally high in complex carbohydrates and fiber and low in sugars, salts, and fats. As possibly the best reflection of general nutritional consciousness, this sound and safe approach to rapid weight loss shows an increasing sophistication among American dieters. The foods in the complex carbohydrates group—grains, vegetables, fruits— are close to nature as well as rich stores of energy. The fiber provides the roughage modern nutritionists have found to be essential to our metabolism of food, and which they believe helps prevent cancer of the colon. Complex carbohydrates have the effect of lowering the blood cholesterol, while fiber helps increase the body's excretion of cholesterol.

This type of diet comes close to the ideal and answers nearly all the requirements a reasonable person could ask of a program that takes off pounds sensibly, and often speedily. The criticism I had of it had nothing to do with its wholesomeness. I quarreled with the "carbohydrates diet" from the standpoint of the *total* eating program, which requires the addition of the good fat. In The Good Fat Diet the extraordinary fish-fat compound *Omega-3* pays long-term health benefits, while the diet itself exemplifies the principle, long recognized by weight-loss experts, that diets that punish don't work. Therefore, in The Good Fat Diet great care has been taken to bring together a rich sampling of the best of fish cuisine in order to promote the desired level of weight loss at a painless and delicious pace.

THE CHEMISTRY OF DIETING

The greater health consciousness among the diets of the eighties is demonstrated in two ways—in their negative approach to fats and in a stricter interpretation of the roles of sugars and salts. In The Good Fat Diet I've incorporated these and other good points of my low-carbohydrate predecessors.

Most of us are aware that sugar interferes with weight loss because this refined, simple carbohydrate makes you fat. Excess sugar is easily converted by the body's metabolism into fat molecules, which are stored as fat in the body's already existing fat cells. Even though there's no disputing this, it's not known why sugar slows the process of losing five, ten, or twenty pounds.

After eating a food high in sugar, we soon experience a "swing" in appetite. This reaction begins because the sugar quickly enters the bloodstream, setting off a surge in the body's insulin production, which causes a rapid decrease in blood sugar levels. This condition signals the brain to stimulate the appetite. Appetite swings are due to the constant bombardment of the brain by signals craving more sugar. We often experience these chemical demands as hunger pangs, which make us think of food. Sugar is the dieter's number one enemy because the appetite swings it induces tend to weaken the will to stick to the diet.

Nearly as useless as sugar, if not in some cases more so, is salt. Every nutritionist today agrees that not only do we eat far more salt than we should (as much as twenty times more than we need in a great many cases), but that we do not need salt at all!

What we do need, nutritionists say, is sodium, and sodium is ingested principally from two sources—the commercial product that we call salt, and in its naturally occurring form that is contained in the foods we eat. Nutritional analysis shows that almost all varieties of foods already contain sodium so that no additional sodium is necessary to sustain the body's metabolic requirements. So salt is really the sodium you add to food, while most of the sodium our body needs is already in the food. The average individual needs about 400 mg of sodium a day. His daily need does not exceed ¹⁄₂₀ teaspoon of table salt. By eating almost any unsalted food, this requirement is more than met, since some sodium is contained in most foods.

The reduction of sodium intake becomes especially important for dieters, since the body uses water to dilute and process sodium, and as it can take the kidneys as long as forty-eight hours to eliminate excess sodium, water is retained and adds to weight. Incidentally, this explains why some overweight people have a bloated appearance; because their diet is overloaded with sodium, a condition is created in which abnormally large amounts of water flow from the cells into the surrounding tissues closer to the body's surface. Because of this change of water concentration levels in the body's external tissues, a puffy appearance emerges.

This does not mean that the dieter does well to abstain from water. On the contrary, the body needs at least six to eight glasses of water a day because water is vital to our bodily metabolism, whether if losing weight is the goal or not. What is at issue is how the body handles water. If the sodium levels are "normal," then the body passes on all the water you drink. At higher sodium levels, the body's tissues retain the water, and we observe the condition of the bloated appearance. A reduction in the intake of sodium is of practical importance to the dieter as well as the nondieter, for water retention leads to high blood pressure and its associated diseases. Most notorious is sodium's association with hypertension, best illustrated by the often cited example of northern Japan where the people consume about 40,000 mg of salt a day, and hypertension is the leading cause of death.

Besides sugar and sodium, another important role in the body's chemistry is played by vitamins and minerals. Vitamins function in body metabolism as an essential part of the enzyme system, while minerals are necessary for the body's growth and development. Seafood is particularly beneficial because it contains large amounts of the necessary mineral iodine. It is also high in the trace mineral zinc, which is not easily obtainable in adequate amounts from other foods. Another mineral found in fish, selenium, is said to help prevent cancer. Fish liver oils are a good source of vitamins A and D. The flesh of fish yields abundant B vitamins, particularly niacin and B-12.

Because of environmental factors, such as pollutants and smoking, as well as nutritive depletion of many foods through processing, the specific need of vitamins and minerals varies with the individual. It can be safely stated, however, that in The Good Fat Diet everything has been done to counter the vitamin/mineral deficiencies of the average high-fat, high-protein American diet, which is lacking in vitamin E, the B complex, vitamin C, calcium, magnesium, and a host of other essential nutrients.

*   *   *

We were fortunate in terms of our dietary aims that the remarkable substance good fat is contained in fish, an already familiar item in rapid-weight-loss programs. On The Good Fat Diet, fish satisfies the necessary fat and protein content most of us expect from a meal.

Study after study has shown that our principal sources of dietary protein like meats and dairy products also contain excessive amounts of the bad saturated fats. These are also responsible for making us the fattest people in the world and leaders in heart disease, for being overweight directly affects the heart—not just the body. On The Good Fat Diet you are losing weight in the interest of heart function through the workings of *Omega-3*.

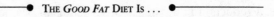

● THE *GOOD FAT* DIET IS ... ●

LOW-CALORIE, LOW-SUGAR, LOW-SALT, LOW-FAT, LOW-PROTEIN. It is "high" in complex carbohydrates, *Omega-3* fish fat, vitamins and minerals, and zest and flavor. Rice, vegetables, fruits (the necessary complement of fiber), fish, lean chicken, the occasional splurge of lean red meat, a dash of "shocking" dessert—the best combination of taste, nutrition, science, and health. A tasty tuna salad for lunch. A "peppy" Cajun-style salmon main dish for dinner ...

It's all in The Good Fat Diet.
It's modern. It works!

6.

How the Wrong Diet Can Cause a Heart Attack

I don't think there's anybody in our country today that is not familiar with the word "cholesterol." Products touted on television talk about it constantly. The American Heart Association bombards us with urgent warnings to decrease our daily intake of this substance, but cholesterol is not only contained in the fatty foods we eat. In fact, cholesterol is manufactured by our body and plays an important and necessary role in its chemical processes.

This vital aspect of cholesterol stands in contrast with its far more publicized menacing role as a factor in heart disease. But a certain amount of cholesterol is crucial in the formation of certain hormones and in the building of cell membranes. Nature has fixed it so that we need no more cholesterol than is manufactured by the body—an amount perfectly adequate to fulfill the body's essential functions. The daily cholesterol content of our diet takes in a punishing 400–800 mg more than we need. Scientists believe that when we obtain too much *dietary* cholesterol, our *blood* cholesterol levels rise above and beyond normal levels, thus causing the scourge of contemporary health problems, cardiovascular disease and the narrowing of the arteries called arteriosclerosis.

Virtually all the plants that supply us with our nutritional needs, the major exceptions being coconut and chocolate, are devoid of cholesterol. The excess we take in comes from animal products, such as meat and dairy items. About half of this unneeded dietary cholesterol is eliminated from the body, but the remainder may be deposited in the inside walls of the arteries, thereby hampering the blood flow through the blood vessels. This is an ongoing process that has been experimentally shown to be initiated in early childhood. At an older age this deposition process results in the bane of modern Americans, arteriosclerosis.

Arteriosclerosis is a "multifactorial disease," that is, it's influenced by heredity, hypertension, diabetes, cigarette smoking, stress, and possible viral injury to the artery walls. Many other factors, in addition, may play a role in its course and development. However, all medical circles are agreed that the chief culprit among all possible factors is the American diet, which has far too much cholesterol and its frequent partner, dietary fats. Therefore, it is advisable that you know your own cholesterol level, as it is an important indicator of the possibility of developing heart disease.

LDL VERSUS HDL

There are two kinds of cholesterol we should be concerned with that are intimately involved in whether or not we will run the risk of heart disease. These are HDL cholesterol (high density lipoprotein) and LDL cholesterol (low density lipoprotein), known as the good and the bad cholesterol, respectively.

—————————• TOTAL CHOLESTEROL (mg/dl) •—————————

	MEN	MODERATE RISK	HIGH RISK
Age	0–14	173	190
	15–19	165	183
	20–29	194	216
	30–39	218	244
	40–49	231	254
	50 and over	230	258
	WOMEN		
	0–14	174	190
	15–19	173	195
	20–29	184	208
	30–39	202	220
	40–49	223	246
	50 and over	252	281

		HDL (mg/dl)	LDL (mg/dl)	
	MEN	INCREASED RISK	MODERATE RISK	HIGH RISK
Age	0–14	38	106	120
	15–19	30	109	123
	20–29	30	128	148
	30–39	29	149	171
	40–49	29	160	180
	50 and over	29	166	188
	WOMEN			
	0–14	36	113	126
	15–19	35	115	135
	20–29	35	127	148
	30–39	35	143	163
	40–49	34	155	177
	50 and over	36	170	195

Arteriosclerosis, or "hardening of the arteries," the most common form of heart disease, has long been known to be associated with LDL and HDL levels. Lipoproteins (HDL and LDL), in fact, exist to carry fats through the bloodstream. LDL is the component branded the bad cholesterol because it is associated with artery and heart trouble. HDL is a good cholesterol because it tries to undo the problems caused by LDL.

The process is easily understood if you visualize LDL as a delivery truck bringing fats to the cells. Too many LDL "carriers" cause them to collide with the artery walls, literally dropping their loads of fat, which then stick to the damaged artery walls in the form of plaque, the process popularly referred to as a clogging of the arteries. HDL, on the other hand, functions more in the nature of a scavenger gathering up excess fats and cholesterol—in effect, "cleaning up" the arteries.

Lowered LDL cholesterol levels have been associated with a reduction in the risk of heart disease. Researchers have seen a lowering of cholesterol levels in patients with increased LDL after putting these patients on a cholesterol-reduced diet. But whereas high LDL cholesterol contributes directly to the development of heart disease, high HDL cholesterol appears to inhibit its development. Clinical studies in Europe have led to similar conclusions. The evidence now overwhelmingly supports dietary methods as the most dramatic way of lowering cholesterol and preventing artery and heart disease. However, some people with a strong hereditary component to high serum cholesterol and LDL may not only require strong dietary restrictions but also pharmaceutical therapy.

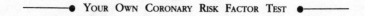 YOUR OWN CORONARY RISK FACTOR TEST

High serum levels of low density lipoprotein (LDL) are found among the rich-food-eating people of Western societies where arteriosclerosis is most prevalent. Those with high serum levels of "scavenger" high density lipoprotein (HDL) have a lower incidence of heart disease. Thus, while your overall cholesterol should be low (below 180; 160 is best), you should also be concerned with the ratio of HDL to total cholesterol. Here's how you can perform your own coronary risk factor test.

From your doctor get your total cholesterol figure and HDL reading. Divide:

$$\frac{\text{TOTAL CHOLESTEROL}}{\text{HDL}}$$

The lower the figure, the better. A ratio of 3.5 is excellent. A ratio between 7 and 9 doubles the standard risk of a heart attack, and a ratio above 12 indicates a 300 percent greater chance of suffering heart disease.

FAT "TRAPS"

When we think of cholesterol we naturally think of fats. There is a definite connection between the two, though not in the way many people think.

Cholesterol is a "sterol," the backbone of many of our important bodily hormones and cell membranes. As mentioned previously, foods high in cholesterol, such as beef and dairy products, at the same time contain high concentrations of fats. Fats and cholesterol go hand and hand in food. Fats are intimately involved in the ultimate amounts of cholesterol in the blood and also other bodily processes that lead to the building up or hardening of the arteries.

LDL cholesterol, the bad cholesterol, is a substance that, when it comes in contact with the artery wall, acts like a magnet attracting deposits, "trapping" the fat that inflames the artery walls. In extremely oversimplified terms, this is the basic mechanism of the hardening process, scientists believe. It means that the interaction between LDL cholesterol and the artery walls results in deposits that are called plaque. The buildup of plaque can eventually plug up an artery so that it can subsequently form a clot (thrombus) that completely blocks the flow of blood. When this occurs we speak of a thrombosis, which may cause a heart attack should the clot form in an artery that conveys blood to the heart. In failing to be nourished by the blood, the heart muscle dies.

It is easy to see, then, that if we wish to get rid of "sludging" fats, we have to drastically cut dietary fat and cholesterol. Many cholesterols and fats are hidden in what we tend to think of as high-protein foods, such as beef or cheese. The high consumption of these foods in our society is one reason why the cholesterol level of the average American is 210 mg, that is, some 50 percent higher than the healthy norm, which results in a 50 percent greater chance of developing heart disease.

The famous Framingham Heart Study has established that serum cholesterol levels above 160 mg are directly related to coronary risk—the higher the value, the higher the risk. Moreover, some scientists also believe cholesterol to be an agent in the development of colon cancer. The data certainly seem to suggest that colon cancer is at its highest in countries with the highest rate of heart disease.

An early warning sign in people with extremely high LDL cholesterol is the skin, which is affected and often forms flat yellowish pimplelike raised surfaces often found on the face or eyelids.

FATS: SATURATED, UNSATURATED

Dietary fats, or fatty acids, by which is meant the fats consumed in our diets, are intimately involved with cholesterol in that they along with proteins are the components of LDL and HDL. Fatty acids can be either saturated or polyunsaturated. So-called saturated fatty acids have a profound effect on raising serum cholesterol; whereas unsaturated fats can actually lower it. Saturated fats also tend to increase the tendency of blood to clot by causing activation of the body's platelet system—the source of the "glue" that makes the fat "stick" to the artery walls. This fact is extremely important in the development of arteriosclerosis.

Our dismal heart disease statistics should not make it surprising to learn that the average American gets 40–50 percent of his calories from fats, with a polyunsaturated to saturated (P/S) fat ratio of 4/10. In other words, for 4 parts of polyunsaturated fat there are 10 parts of saturated fat in our food-fat intake. Public policymakers have recommended that this figure should be down to about 15/10, or for every 15 parts of polyunsaturated fat there should be only 10 parts of saturated fat consumed.

What this indicates, among other things, is that a higher polyunsaturated fat intake is obviously preferable to that consisting of saturated fat. For one thing, polyunsaturated fatty acids have long been considered essential to proper nutrition and growth. Vegetables, fish, and poultry happen to contain high concentrations of this good fat. In other words, as researchers have emphatically stated, it is not just the amount of fat in the diet, but the *type* of fat that matters. For instance, one experiment clearly demonstrated that feeding two vegetable fats (coconut oil, a saturated fat, and corn oil, an unsaturated fat) resulted in vastly different cholesterol levels: Coconut oil raises cholesterol; whereas corn oil lowers it. It has only been within the last thirty years that this relationship—the cholesterol-lowering effects of polyunsaturated fats present in vegetable oils—has become understood.

Our body provides most of the essential fats we need, except one, the polyunsaturated fat called linoleic acid, which must be provided by the diet. Except for fish and poultry, animal foods are low in linoleic acid, which happens to be the most useful nutrient. The body requires linoleic acid for many of its essential metabolic functions including the manufacture of molecules called prostaglandins that facilitate the most basic cell communications. Early studies showed that substitutions of polyunsaturated fat in the form of linoleic acid actually reduces cholesterol levels in normal, healthy people. Moreover, in recent years higher intake of this good fat has been recommended to prevent heart disease.

THE RISE AND FALL OF CHOLESTEROL

The rise and fall of serum cholesterol levels is a direct measure of the type of foods we eat. The level is raised by a low-fiber diet dominated by animal fats and protein, that is, the kind of meal we get from egg yolks, butter, and red meat, which makes our blood cells "stick" together.

The Good Fat Diet, an eating program incorporating complex carbohydrates, fiber, vegetables, and the "miracle fish," containing Omega-3, has low levels of cholesterol and is low in fat, resulting in a significant drop of the cholesterol level.

One could expect a drop of up to 20–30 percent in serum cholesterol levels within a month of changing from a fat-rich diet to The Good Fat Diet. The Good Fat Diet has helped my family's serum cholesterol levels drop below 180. This is identical to the people living in societies where there is limited use of rich foods—the same societies where heart disease is rare. We like looking slim. We love our low-cholesterol, low-calorie way of eating. But it's even more splendid to know that the heart is getting all the oxygen it needs, functioning unimpeded by fat-clogged poundage and "sludged-up" arteries.

Researchers have also found that a diet without cholesterol slows down the growth of cancer in animals. There is now some evidence that fats increase the development of certain cancers in people, for instance cancer of the colon, kidneys, ovaries, and prostate. A high consumption of fat is also being related to breast cancer.

Other animal experiments have shown this type of low-fat, low-cholesterol diet to be capable of reversing the hardening of the arteries. Studies on humans have shown a correlated drop in cholesterol with the possible reversal of arteriosclerosis in the arteries that feed the heart.

——————● WHAT'S YOUR FAT CALORIE COUNT? ●——————

Strict disciplinarians among nutritionists advocate a fat intake of no more than 5 percent. This is an unusually severe approach and probably impracticable if not unhealthy. The benchmark in The Good Fat Diet is a fat content considerably lower than the American Heart Association's "prudent" 35 percent. I believe, along with the conclusions reached by Senate hearings on the subject, that 20 percent of total calories as fat is the safest and most realistic of the generally recommended figures to support a healthful life, free from the specter of bad-fat-related diseases.

THE CAVEMAN DIET

Studies have shown that heart disease is rare among people with low cholesterol concentrations and high among societies such as ours, where the cholesterol concentrations are phenomenal by normal standards. In fact, what we have come to accept as normal cholesterol levels are unquestionably high levels for the human species. This means that our current diet oversupplies the body with unnecessary and heart-threatening amounts of fats and cholesterol. This seems to suggest that most heart problems are *not* entirely genetic in origin. They are influenced by the diet we get from our environment.

Scientists have come up with fascinating findings when comparing the modern diet to that of our ancestors the cavemen. Like us, our prehistoric forebears obtained food from their environment. We have essentially the same genetic code they had. Like the hearts of our remote ancestors, ours too require nonstop functioning. The heart does not regenerate as a muscle, and once a portion of it dies, the task of contracting 103,000 times a day places an extraordinary burden on whatever part of the cardiac muscle survives. We are today still genetically programmed for the diets available to the caveman.

Truly modern human beings, Homo sapiens, first appeared about 40,000 years ago. As a genus, humanity has existed for about 2 million years, with our prehuman hominid ancestor, australopithecus, having appeared about 4 million years ago. By studying this evolutionary process from a nutritional standpoint, and by observing today's primitive cultures, scientists have been able to speculate what the caveman ate. While much more vulnerable in other ways, the caveman was found in terms of nutrition to be better adapted to his environment. These findings give dramatic evidence that what we eat in a twentieth-century industrialized society has an obvious impact on our health.

The specific pattern of our modern nutritionally inspired scourges—coronary heart disease, hypertension, cancer, and diabetes—is actually a function of the stage of our civilization. These scourges are hardly known to the few so-called primitive societies still extant in Africa today. Researchers theorize that the full onset of our modern health problems has only been felt during the past 100 years, when we first adopted our current dietary habits. What it comes down to essentially is that the body is unable to efficiently metabolize our virtual overdose on animal fat and cholesterol. It has been suggested that our modern unprecedented incidence of heart disease and cancer is due to the longer life expectancy in industrialized countries. However, young-sters living in the Western countries commonly show early signs of heart disease, unlike youths living in preagricultural African societies, who do not suffer from certain deficiencies found in the modern "civilized" diet.

WILD FAT

Today's surviving primitive societies have little heart disease, scientists believe, because they eat wild animal fat. We obtain our fat from domesticated animals. Domesticated animals have always been fatter than their wild ancestors. In fact, the meat available in the modern American supermarket may be said to be "super-fat," with an in-creased portion of fat as the result of the demand for tender meat. Because of this consumer choice the modern animal breed-ing and feeding practices enable the production of high-fat car-casses with more than 30 percent fat. Compare this to the findings of a study of fifteen different species of free-living African herbivores that came up with an average fat content of barely 4 percent.

Heart attacks were extremely rare in the United States and Great Britain until about sixty years ago. Even obesity until modern times affected only the wealthy, who could afford a diet richer in fats. Scientists explain the virtual absence of obesity and heart problems among primitives as being due not only to a diet low in fat, but as well to a diet in which the fats have a different composition from those of meats we buy at the supermarket. Primitives appear to consume less total fat and more good fat than bad fat. Remarkably, *Omega-3* is also found in high concentrations in the wild game they hunt, just as worlds away the Eskimo obtains his from the fish he consumes.

For reasons not fully understood by scientists, today's domesti-cated animals, which give us our tender meat, not only have more fat but also the worst kind of fat, the bad saturated fat. The fat the cavemen obtained from wild game contained per gram over five times more polyunsaturated fats. Good fat is still found in wild game. The meat from undomesticated animals contains *Omega-3* fatty acids de-rived not from marine but from plant life.

It is almost paradoxical that the sophisticated fish recipes devel-oped for the good fat weight-loss program in this book have an affinity with the Eskimo and caveman diet.

7.

The Secret of Omega-3

To understand what *Omega-3* is all about, what it does and why the human body needs it, I must again talk a little more about fats, but happily it will be about good fats, that is, the polyunsaturated kind.

As everybody who shops for food and reads about diets knows, these fats have been a part of our life since the early fifties. At that time high cholesterol levels were first associated with a high incidence of coronary heart disease. As a result of these alarming dietary findings, the Western world was undergoing its first scare about cholesterol and dietary fats. Suddenly vegetable oils and margarine were marked with new distinctions, "polyunsaturated" and "low cholesterol."

The particular polyunsaturated fat first hailed in the fifties was known by its chemical name as *Omega-6* or linoleic acid. It belonged to the family of unsaturated fatty acids that include the similarly named linolenic acid (*Omega-3*) and oleic acid (*Omega-9*).

─────────● HERE'S WHAT GOOD FAT LOOKS LIKE: ●─────────

Omega-9 $H_3C—C—C—C—C—C—C—C—\overset{9}{C}=$
(monosaturated fat)   C-RCOOH

Omega-6 $H_3C—C—C—C—C—\overset{6}{C}$ = C-R'COOH
(polyunsaturated fat)

Omega-3 $H_3C—C—\overset{3}{C} = C\text{-}R''COOH$
(polyunsaturated good fat)

Omega is the last letter of the Greek alphabet. The three major families of fatty acids that are most important in human nutrition are named *Omega-3, -6, and -9*. The numbering is based on the actual physical location of the first double bond (designated: =) counting from the left end of the carbon atoms on the fatty acid chain.

Imagine the different types of fatty acids as being similar to chains in which carbon atoms are strung together. Each carbon atom in *saturated* (bad fat) fatty acid is usually linked to its neighboring carbon atom by a *single* bond, its chemical connector. In contrast, the unsaturated fatty acid chains have a *double* bond in each chain at the 3, 6, or 9 position, which determines the respective nomenclature. On the microbiological level the location of these double bonds ultimately determines the way in which each of these different fatty acids affects our body chemistry.

It has only been in the past few decades that scientists have begun to understand the significance of the carbon chain. From a nutritional standpoint this has meant a remarkable advance in that now scientists can study what people eat and at the same time look at it on the molecular level. In this region visible only to the trained eye and through special chemical techniques, scientists found that *Omega-3* was a special kind of fat that is concentrated in fish oil. Long hailed in folklore as "brain food," fish was now proven as well to have a vital influence on the smooth functioning and preservation of the heart.

THE TWO FACES OF FAT

Both *Omega-6* and *Omega-3* are regarded in medical terminology as EFA, essential fatty acids, because the body cannot manufacture them and they can only come from outside food sources. The principal and best characterized EFA is linoleic acid, the *Omega-6*. A dietary intake of 1–2 percent of total calories as linoleic acid is regarded as sufficient to prevent EFA deficiency, an amount that is easily obtained from our normal eating patterns, since much of what we consume, including vegetables, whether fresh or processed, contains this fat.

Precisely how linoleic acid participates in human nutrition has become clearer through recent research, which has associated *one* of its functions as stimulating the production of arachidonic acid, a molecule from which prostaglandins are derived. We have already mentioned prostaglandins in the previous chapter. Prostaglandins are a diverse group of molecules which can mediate inflammation, widen or constrict blood vessels, and thus, in a real sense, exercise control over the flow of blood to the heart and other vital organs.

Among the essential fatty acids, *Omega-6* had been considered sufficient until recently, when scientists discovered that the human body appeared to need *Omega-3* as well. It almost seemed from their glowing reports that everything *Omega-6* could do, *Omega-3* could do better. For instance, *Omega-6* was long known for its ability to lower cholesterol and LDL levels, which, as we know, are directly associated with heart attacks. However, not only does *Omega-3* perform to the same effect, but it has in addition anticlotting properties that interfere with the self-destructive heart attack mechanism. Studies have actually shown spectacular results of *Omega-3* when consumed in lowering cholesterol, triglycerides, and LDL in patients with abnormally high blood fats some three to four times the normal range.

The scientists observing this and other astonishing facets of *Omega-3* realized that not only was it structurally distinct from *Omega-6*, but it was, as far as concerned its effects on humans, an altogether different *type* of fat—a fat that was beneficial to people, especially those at high risk for heart disease. One of the extraordinary properties of this fat, found in significant quantities in fish, is that it prevents the blood from "sticking."

More has since become known about the amazing good fat. Scientists had partially unlocked the secret of *Omega-3*. Their efforts were spurred on by the great promise for modern man's health held out by the mysterious molecule that actually combats cholesterol.

TURF AND SURF

The difference between *Omega-6* and *Omega-3* is the difference between "turf and surf." It is at the level of infinitesimal atomic structures that the distinction arises between the meat and seafood on our plates. Bearing this in mind, what must be remembered about

Omega-6 and *Omega-3* is that they are molecules belonging to the same family.

At the very start of the molecular process we find them sharing a common denominator in that both derive from plants. Seeds and leaves are the principal sources of both linoleic (*Omega-6*) and linolenic (*Omega-3*) acids. But there are plants that grow on land and plants that grow on the murky floor of the ocean; and of the two polyunsaturated fatty acids, *Omega-6* originates in the cellular processes of seeds and leaves of the earth, while *Omega-3* forms at the great marine tree of life that weaves beneath the waters.

Omega-3 derives from phytoplankton, which is at the bottom of the marine food chain. Accordingly, scientists say, all other forms of marine life eventually become enriched with *Omega-3* fatty acids, including fish. Scientists believe that *Omega-3* fatty acids provide fish with the required degree of unsaturation to allow fish membranes to remain fluid in frigid water.

EICOSANOIDS

To biochemists, the key to understanding the good fat lies in the process of prostaglandin metabolism. Prostaglandins are molecules said to influence the widening and narrowing of the blood vessels. They are believed to mediate the inflammatory process. The distinct enzyme (cycloxygenase) that produces prostaglandin imparts to it the effect of stimulating inflammation and smooth muscle contraction. Aspirin, for example, blocks prostaglandin synthesis—hence aspirin's anti-inflammatory properties.

Prostaglandin is a member of the family of a class of compounds, the eicosanoids. A number of studies have shown that *Omega-3* appears to have a modulating effect on certain eicosanoids, and because eicosanoids have broad inflammatory effects—heart disease is classified "inflammatory"—their curtailment by *Omega-3* fatty acids can halt the progress of these crippling diseases.

One of the leading experts on *Omega-3*, William Lands, head of biological chemistry at the University of Illinois in Chicago, sees all such inflammatory diseases as the consequence of "exaggerated eicosanoid signals." He sees the eicosanoids as local regulators, which communicate in chemical signals—the cells, as it were, "chattering" back and forth with one another. In order to unlock the secret of

Omega-3, scientists had to be able to listen in to this chemical language of the eicosanoids and try to understand the significance of these molecular voices, some shouting loudly, others merely whispering, or not speaking at all. Heart disease, then, appears to come about as the result of the wrong message passed by the eicosanoids to the cells, or a message that is not heard. One mistake, says Lands, can be blown out of all proportion by positive feedback mechanisms. Consequently, there is confusion, and the confusion, as it always does, multiplies.

Eicosanoids are produced in the body from polyunsaturated fatty acids derived from the diet. Astonishingly, however, it appears, according to Lands and other biochemists, that *Omega-3* generated eicosanoids are distinctly less inflammatory than the *Omega-6* generated eicosanoids. When stimulated, by an injury, for instance, eicosanoids synthesized by *Omega-6* will rise "explosively" to very high concentrations, according to Lands, much higher than concentrations of eicosanoids synthesized from *Omega-3* fatty acids. *Omega-3* keeps the more "inflammatory" molecules from acting, scientists now say. It is known that increased consumption of *Omega-3* fatty acids increases the ratio of *Omega-3* to *Omega-6* in all the components of human blood. Scientists who recommend adding fish oils to our diet claim that the special benefits of these marine fats are due to the increased ratio of *Omega-3* in the composition.

Omega-3 plays the role of subtly altering the inflammatory process. Biochemists point out that in atherosclerosis the arteries do not "harden" overnight; the lethal cholesterols and fats seeking to imbed in the eicosanoid-produced inflammations do not "sludge up" the arterial walls after one fat-rich meal. The eating habits of a lifetime go into the building of the thickened walls of the arteries that cause a heart attack or stroke. Advanced medical opinion agrees that because heart disease is a step-by-step process, it can be interfered with and slowed—and possibly reversed—by the special fatty acid, *Omega-3,* that decreases serum cholesterol and LDL levels, and subtly alters platelet function and eicosanoid chemistry. Thus, there is reduced risk that fatty deposits will form in the arteries.

SCIENTISTS PRAISE *OMEGA-3*

Some of us have perhaps had a grandmother who tormented us at bedtime with a spoonful of cod-liver oil. We now know the wisdom contained in this item of folklore. Grandmother knew nothing about *Omega-3* as the double bond on the third atom of the carbon chain. She was simply acting in blind obedience to traditional custom that dictated that fish oils were good for you. It is interesting then to know about a full-scale conference attended by many of America's foremost biochemists that appeared to corroborate grandmother's instinctive wisdom. The conference took place in 1984 in Washington, D.C., and its prime topic, dominating the discussion, was the effect and impact of *Omega-3* on the human body.

The scientists at the conference engaged in sometimes heated controversy over the recommended levels of *Omega-3* consumption. By far, however, most seemed convinced that an increased content of these fatty acids in human tissues will reduce the incidence of coronary heart disease. They praised the U.S. Health and Human Services Department and U.S. Agricultural Department for their current recommendation of as many as *four* fish meals a week. They described it as a hopeful sign as regards the nutritional goal of raising the average person's one fish meal a week to at least two.

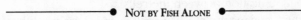

● NOT BY FISH ALONE ●

Not every kind of fish meal serves the same role as a nutritional booster. The type of fish served in fast-food establishments is actually *less* nutritious when compared with other fast foods like chicken or hamburger. In fact, a fast-food fish sandwich is higher in fat than either a four-ounce hamburger or a light meat chicken entrée. The fast-food fish sandwich is nearly one-third lower in protein than either chicken or hamburger. The breading and frying of most fast-food seafoods increase the total fat content. A fast-food fish sandwich is even higher in cholesterol than a quarter-pound hamburger!

FAT AND CHOLESTEROL COMPARISON OF FAST FOODS

FAST FOOD	FAT (gm)	CHOLESTEROL (mg)	CALORIES
Fish Sandwich	15.7	53	276
Chicken Entrée (light meat)	14.2	95	263
Hamburger (4-ounce patty)	12.1	41	255
Cheeseburger (4-ounce patty)	16.2	54	270

One of the most exciting topics to be discussed during the Washington, D.C., *Omega-3* conference dealt with the newest findings concerning the anticlotting properties of *Omega-3*, which is helpful in the prevention of thrombosis, a mechanism involving primarily platelets and clotting factors.

Platelets are the cell-like structures in the blood that initiate blood clots. In its normal functions the body uses these platelets to stop bleeding after injury. Though these platelets are essential after injury in preventing the victim from bleeding to death, occasions may arise that due to certain dietary conditions something goes wrong in the chemical communication between the cells.

When that happens the mechanism becomes harmful. It becomes a deadly problem, for instance, when a coronary artery narrowed by years of fat deposits on its walls suddenly ruptures. The sudden break initiates the body's clotting process. Millions of platelets now come rushing into the artery with its narrowed walls. Soon the number of the platelets is too great, creating a plug that stops blood flow to the heart. The reduced blood flow causes a thrombosis, a heart attack, and inevitably results in part of the heart muscle dying.

Scientists now believe that the positive effects of fish fat occur because of the apparent interference of *Omega-3* with the normal metabolism and function of platelets. They believe that the remarkable workings of *Omega-3* on platelet function through *Omega-3*'s action on eicosanoid chemistry, may slow the process of fat deposits in the artery walls over the course of years.

It was found that the people on high *Omega-3* diets had platelets that were less "sticky" and aggregated less easily than platelets in "normal" blood. Consequently, the fats and cholesterol that perform their nutritional functions by circulating in the blood are less likely to stick to the walls of the arteries, resulting in less narrowing of the blood vessels, all of which means less chance that the arteries will be blocked by subsequent formation of a life-threatening thrombosis.

THE STRANGE TALE OF UMANAK

The remarkable effects of *Omega-3* on the human chemistry were first studied in depth on a people who ironically live primarily on fats and whose dietary habits have been hardly influenced by "civilization." This rare sample consisted of the natives of Umanak. As Eskimos, they belonged to the most carnivorous people on earth, with a diet consisting of seal, whale, and fish, which they hunted and fished in their bleak homeland some 300 miles north of the polar circle on Greenland's barren west coast.

Their fat intake, enormous by Western standards, should have assured every native of death from heart disease, since, as we know, a high consumption of animal fat raises the level of serum cholesterol, which is strongly correlated to atherosclerotic disease, especially heart disease. Nevertheless, about thirty years ago reports began to reach the scientific community that the serum cholesterol level in Eskimos was lower than that of the population of Western Europe, and that their incidence of heart disease was very low. This puzzling anomaly led two young Danish scientists, Bang and Dyerberg, to mount in 1970 a two-month-long expedition to Umanak, from which they returned with the astonishing findings that have since revolutionized nutritional thinking.

EXTRAORDINARY CONTRADICTION

The two Danish scientists followed for one week the complete eating cycle of an equal number of male and female Greenlanders in the remote settlement of Umanak. The Eskimo food consisted of a monotonous high-fat eating regimen of seal, whale, and fish. Fat intake could go as high as 600 g a day. The mammoth intake of high-fat meat gave the Eskimos an average daily consumption of cholesterol as high as 400–800 mg, almost double that of the Danes. But at the same time the concentrations of cholesterol, triglycerides, and LDL (low density lipoprotein) were found to be much lower in the Eskimos. The extraordinary contradiction—high dietary fats and low blood fats—so much the opposite of what one would expect, was made all the more inconsistent by the much higher levels of HDL (high density lipoprotein), the good cholesterol. The HDL levels of the Eskimos with their high-fat dietary pattern were found to be much higher than that of their counterparts in Denmark.

A number of scientists had already established that HDL reduces the risk of heart disease, and in fact, the Bang-Dyerberg study of the Eskimo diet was one of the first to confirm by the evidence of an actual field study with human participants the association between a high level of HDL and a low incidence of heart disease. When first published, some scientists argued that the paradoxical findings at Umanak might be due to racial peculiarities in the Eskimo metabolism of fats. But this was disproven by further evidence that the blood lipid levels of Eskimos living in Denmark were discovered to be at the same high risk for heart disease as their Danish neighbors. In effect, their lipid patterns were similar to the Danes'. There was no correlation between race and metabolism of fats.

Since high LDL levels are typical of individuals with artery disease, in finding neither present in the high-fat-consuming Eskimos, scientists were led to conclude that something in their food consumption was suppressing the LDL formation. This was explained by the Eskimo diet, which they said contained large amounts of the *Omega-3* fatty acids.

● OMEGA-3 CONTENT OF SELECTED FISH ●
(per 100 grams)

More than 1.0 gram:

Sockeye salmon	2.7
Albacore tuna	2.1
King salmon	1.9
Atlantic mackerel	1.9
Bluefin tuna	1.5

Pink salmon	1.5
Coho salmon	1.5
Anchovy	1.4
Lake trout	1.4
Atlantic salmon	1.4
Sablefish	1.3
Atlantic halibut	1.3
American eel	1.2
Sardine	1.2
Pacific herring	1.2
Atlantic herring	1.2
Pacific mackerel	1.1
Cisco	1.1
Rainbow trout	1.1

0.6 to 1.0 gram:

Swordfish	0.9
Striped bass	0.7
Turbot	0.7
Yellowfin tuna	0.6
Red snapper	0.6
Channel catfish	0.6

0.5 gram and under:

Pacific halibut	0.5
Carp	0.5
Ocean perch	0.4
Brook trout	0.3
Rockfish	0.3
Sturgeon	0.2
Yellowtail	0.2
Haddock	0.2
Yellow perch	0.2
Walleye	0.2
Atlantic cod	0.2
Pacific cod	0.1
Northern pike	0.1
Sole	0.1

As far back as the 1930s a French explorer visiting northern Canadian Eskimos noted among them a surprising bruising or bleeding tendency. In 1940, another researcher noted frequent nosebleeds among the Eskimos of Greenland. Among the tests the two Danish scientists performed on the natives of Umanak during the 1970s was one that measured their bleeding time, which they found to be prolonged—though not to any harmful extent—in comparison to a control group of Eskimos living in Denmark. This led to the chief breakthrough in understanding *Omega-3*'s antinarrowing, anticlotting properties.

In biochemical terms, the prolonged bleeding time of the Eskimos has been explained as being due to a change in platelet fatty acid composition. Platelets, remember, are directly involved in both the long-term deadly formation of plaque on the artery walls, as well as in the ultimate formation of the "plug" (thrombus) that causes the heart attack. Scientists now theorize that fish-eating people show a suppressed platelet activity (a lessening of the blood's tendency to clot), due to *Omega-3* action as a neutralizer of certain prostaglandins (a type of eiconsanoid) the "inflammatory" chemical catalysts of the heart disease process. What happens, they believe, is that tissues normally high in prostaglandin-related substances become overwhelmed and saturated with *Omega-3*. Hence the prolonged bleeding time of the Eskimos.

THE *OMEGA-3* IMPERATIVE

Most dieters already know that meat as a source of protein is more fat-dense than fish. A four-ounce piece of fish is typically half the calories of a four-ounce piece of meat, and has far less fat. For dieting purposes, few sources of low-calorie protein are as rich as seafoods. A three-and-one-half-ounce portion of white fish, for example, is low in fat, has less than 100 calories, and supplies about one-third of an adult's Recommended Dietary Allowance of protein. This explains in part why the fish-eating people of the Asian nations are thinner than a predominantly red-meat-eating society. Fish is proverbial diet food, famed for its capacity to bring quick weight-loss results. But outweighing this practical advantage of fish for the dieter, it was the far-reaching biomedical and health implications connected with the latest findings regarding fish that made The Good Fat Diet a *necessity* to modern men and women.

It is not just for those wishing to lose weight or maintain it at the desired level. Nor is it exclusively for those who simply like the

Omega-3 diet recipes from the great fish kitchens of the world. The Good Fat Diet is for everyone interested in preventing or halting his own risk of heart disease.

The findings among the *Omega-3*–eating Eskimos are of extreme significance to none more so than the rich fat-consuming Western nations. Although from a purely scientific standpoint it is not recommended that people continue their high-fat dietary life-styles, theoretically the discovery of the positive effects of *Omega-3* on preventing heart disease indicates that even if an individual continues with the American-style high-fat food consumption—without lowering, in other words, the fat content—the mere addition of fish to this "killer" regimen may provide the body with enough *Omega-3* to significantly lower the risk of heart disease. What this means is that The Good Fat Diet offers hope even for a person unable to shake the high cholesterol habit, for by adding *Omega-3*–bearing fish to his usual food intake, he need not necessarily get "fat on the inside."

The *Good Fat* Diet calls for a general reduction of fats in our diet from the current average of 35–40 percent to an ideal of 20 percent. But even if the dieter falls short of reaching this ideal low of dietary fat content, his consumption of fish rich in *Omega-3* may be enough in and of itself to reduce the chance of heart disease.

It's also possible to use the recipes in The *Good Fat* Diet for a "crash" course to lower your body's serum cholesterol levels—provided you consult your doctor first. One study done at the University of Oregon showed a dramatic drop in cholesterol levels by up to 17 percent in normal volunteers, with the drop registered in patients with elevated cholesterol as much as 20 percent, while they were on a ten-day diet of salmon containing *Omega-3* fatty acids. While salmon is not the only fish that contains *Omega-3,* it has been used in nutrition studies of this nature because it is the richest fish source of this *good fat.*

● THE MYTH OF LOBSTER ●

Although lobster has gained a bad reputation for being rich in cholesterol, actual analysis has shown it to be relatively low in cholesterol, about 70 milligrams per 100 grams. This amount of cholesterol is comparatively insignificant—virtually the same as for swordfish or trout. Apart from squid and certain varieties of crab, most shellfish don't deserve the popular high cholesterol stigma with which they have been associated.

● CHOLESTEROL CONTENT OF SELECTED FISH AND SHELLFISH ●

Salmon	35*
Tuna	38
Clams, softshell	25
Clams, hardshell	40
Swordfish	48
Oysters, all species	50
Shrimp	66
Trout, brook	68
Lobster	70
Crab	78
Squid	250

*All measures are in milligrams per 100 grams. Almost all fish and shellfish are very low in cholesterol and may contain no cholesterol at all. Those fish that do contain cholesterol typically contain amounts commensurate with those listed above.

How effective even a diet partially containing *Omega-3* fats from fish can be has been convincingly demonstrated by studies done in Holland and Japan. Both studies were significant in that they did not involve a people still leading the primitive hunter-fisherman existence of the natives of Umanak, but two advanced modern peoples.

In the developed world the Japanese are unique for having a high intake of *Omega-3* from fresh fish, which scientists now say may in part contribute to their low incidence of cardiovascular disease. But there is an interesting heart disease statistic about this nation of fish eaters. The population living on the island of Okinawa has the highest consumption of fish in all of Japan. They also have the lowest incidence of heart disease among the entire Japanese population.

On the other hand, the study done in Holland bears on the issue about not getting "fat on the inside" by means of even a modest addition of *Omega-3* fish to the normal intake of fats. In a twenty-year study of the relation of fish consumption to heart disease, the Dutch found that the death rate from its causes was over 50 percent lower among those who consumed at least 30 g of fish per day than among those who did not eat fish. From these results it was concluded that eating as little as one or two fish dishes per week may be of preventive value to coronary heart disease.

8.

"Catch of the Day": Shopping for the Right Fish

Americans' interest in eating fish, a broadening of the palate, and a greater variety of fish being served and sold led me to the cuisines of many other countries for inspiration in creating recipes for The Good Fat Diet. But the first task was to familiarize myself with the basics. What are the differences among the species for flavor, texture, *Omega-3* content? Where to shop for fish? What kind of fish? How much fish? Fresh fish? Frozen fish? What is meant by "whole" or "drawn," "filleted" or "steaked" fish? I learned that fish is a remarkably versatile food and by shopping for, buying, and cooking fish as part of our life-style, I easily succeeded in becoming adept at cooking delicious and healthy meals.

When I first began visiting fish markets and fish sections at the supermarkets, I acquainted myself with the different varieties of fish and a new terminology. I learned which fish best lent itself to go with what spices and condiments; whether to use in preparing it the "moist method" (poaching, steaming) or the "dry method" (baking, broiling, grilling). I trained myself to inspect a fish for its quality and freshness. In addition, though in The Good Fat Diet I sought to combine a high-complex carbohydrate program with a dietary program centered around fish, it was not just any or all of the hundreds of species currently being marketed in the United States that qualified for inclusion.

The flesh of fish, both freshwater and saltwater, generally recommends itself to a low-fat diet food, since it is low in sodium content and supplies many minerals, such as calcium, iron, potassium, along with important vitamins, such as the B complex vitamins. Most fish share the characteristic of being "lighter" and more easily digestible than animal meats. The fish for the diet, however, were the good fat fish, which, in addition to the acknowledged nutrient qualities shared by all fish, were distinguished for having the compound *Omega-3*.

Many of the dishes on The Good Fat Diet look so good, it sometimes comes as a shock to people that this low-fat diet food is also good for you. The secret is to cook fish with spices, vegetables, and fruits, which impart so much flavor to the dish that the salt, sugars, bad fats, and bad cholesterol are no longer missed; hence the body no longer craves them. Fish is most responsive to flavoring while being cooked. Some kinds of fish require special flavors to offset somewhat neutral natural flavors. Others need no more than a dash of pepper to bring out a richness in taste that may be enhanced with a glass of light white wine.

I was fortunate that in developing The Good Fat Diet I had a school that was as large and culinary wise as multinational southern California itself, where peoples from the Asian fish-eating nations in particular have contributed their distinctive flavors to what's become the new California "light" trend in eating. This trend uses the ethnic gourmet secrets from L.A.'s overseas newcomers, a number of simple techniques and methods that are responsible for making their foods so tasty and satisfying.

BUYING FISH

When buying fish, remember that fat content varies according to species. Herring is a fatter fish than rainbow trout. Members of the cod family have less than 1 percent fat, while salmon and mackerel have as much as 20–25 percent. But here a fish high in fat, such as salmon, is high in the good fat. It has more *Omega-3*, and thus we have the paradox that a fish low in fat like cod is not as suitable for The Good Fat Diet.

Most fish is low in calories. Consult the fish calorie chart on pages 171–74 before shopping. As to how much fish you should buy, go by the rule that you will need about one-third to one-half pound per person. Generally, an eight-ounce portion should satisfy the average adult. This means *edible* fish, and does not include the bones, head, tail, and so on. When buying a whole fish, count on buying about one pound per person. While on the rapid-weight-loss program of The Good Fat Diet, plan on about one-half pound per person. Once you return to a higher calorie regimen than The Good Fat Diet calls for, make sure to incorporate at least two fish meals a week in your dietary program in order to maintain your weight loss and continue to help protect your heart against damage.

THE FISH-BUYING VOCABULARY

The first thing to think about is *how much* you need when buying:

• *Whole-dressed fish*—Allow one pound per serving, except for red snapper; allow one and one-quarter pounds per serving for the snapper, since its large head makes up about half its weight. For stuffing a whole fish, the per-pound allowance should be decreased proportionately.

• *Pan-dressed fish*—Generally allow half a pound for each person. To be on the safe side, however, since the amount of meat may vary after skin and bones are removed, tell your fishman the number of people to be fed and ask his advice.

• *Steaks*—Here waste is at a minimum, so one pound may serve two or three persons, depending on how hungry they are.

• *Fillets*—One pound usually serves two or three people, especially when combined with a filling complement.

● SAY IT LOUD AND CLEAR ●

There was the person who asked her fish dealer for two pounds of bass *fillet,* and the fishman, hearing two pounds of bass *filleted,* proceeded to fillet the fish until the hapless buyer was left with fourteen ounces of bass to feed five people. Use the word "net weight" when consulting your fishman and tell him how many will be dining. There are great variations among the "net weights" fish will yield. For instance, around spawning time the roe enlarges to the extent of taking up as much as one-fifth of fish body weight. Some fish have fragile bones, others have heavy skeletons. A four-pound red snapper, because of its large head, will yield at most two pounds of edible meat. A four-pound bass will yield about three pounds. On the other hand, as many as ten or twelve people may dine off four pounds of sole fillets when cooked and served with a sauce including other food ingredients.

The shopper for fish soon learns a new terminology having to do with the various market forms of fish. Here, for instance, "dressed" means "cleaned." You and your fishmonger will be speaking the same language if you use the following vocabulary in identifying the form in which you wish to buy fish:

• *Whole or round*—Whole fish, just as it comes to dockside from the water. However, when a recipe calls for whole fish it usually means "whole dressed."

• *Whole dressed*—Whole fish scaled and gutted, that is, with the insides removed. Fins are removed; head and tail normally remain. The backbone also remains, but ask to have it taken out if you plan to stuff the fish.

• *Drawn*—Drawn fish differs from whole fish only in having its entrails removed. It is gutted through a small neck slit, leaving the fish itself unsplit, so that with the head, tail, scales, fins, and gills removed it can subsequently be cut into any other form. The milt or roe, the male and female reproductive glands, usually remain.

• *Pan dressed*—It's the same whole-dressed fish scaled and gutted but with the head and tail removed. This is most popular for all small fish, since they are then ready for any cooking method. (However, with very small fish such as smelt, the head and tail are usually not removed.)

• *Steaks*—Cross-cut slices of a drawn or dressed fish, ideally one-half- to one-and-one-half inches thick. The piece of the backbone each slice contains should be left intact. Many of the larger species—tuna, halibut, white sea bass, salmon, and swordfish—appear in this form. Two other cuts of steak are loin steaks (rounded in shape) and rib steaks (cross-cut pieces taken along the body cavity).

• *Fillets*—Sides of dressed fish cut lengthwise, parallel to the backbone, with the skin on or removed, depending on the recipe. A large fillet divided in two is known as "cross-cut" fillets, which when in turn cut in two gives "quarter-cut fillets." Fillets are virtually free of bones.

• *Butterfly fillets*—Fillet with the skin left on and uncut along the back, so that the two fillets remain attached ventrally.

• *Fish sticks*—Rectangular fish strips cut from a block of frozen fillets and usually sold frozen.

The basis of many fish recipes is a good fish stock. When buying a whole fish filleted, ask for the head, carcass, skin, bones, and other parts for making stock. Simmered with fresh vegetables, the stock can be strained and used for sauces and seafood stews present in The Good Fat Diet. Usually fish dealers give trimmings away, or else you can buy them for pennies.

Fish stock such as is made, for example, from poached salmon is delicious. It is easy to make and economical. It can be frozen and kept a long time. Clam juice, often used instead of fish stock, is far inferior to the real thing, though it'll do in a pinch.

—————● FLAVOR AND TEXTURE CHARACTERISTICS OF SELECTED FISH* ●—————

FISH	FLAVOR	TEXTURE
Black sea bass	3	3
Striped bass	4	1
Bluefish	4	2
Catfish	2	3
Catfish, ocean	3	4
Cod	3	3
Eel	3	5
Flounder	1	1
Haddock	2	3
Halibut	3	4
Herring	5	3
Mackerel	5	2

*This chart represents a general range of measurements for both the flavor and texture of the most widely available fish in today's marketplace. The higher numbers like 4 and 5 indicate the strongest flavors and textures. The lower numbers indicate milder flavors and more delicate textures of fish.

Fish	Flavor	Texture
Mahimahi	2	4
Monkfish	3	4
Perch, ocean	2	3
Pike	1	3
Pollack, Atlantic	4	4
Pompano	2	3
Red Snapper	3	4
Rockfish	2	3
Sablefish	3	3
Salmon	5	4
Shark	3	5
Smelt	3	3
Sole	1	1
Swordfish	4	5
Trout	3	3
Tuna	4	5
Turbot, Greenland	1	1
Whitefish	2	2

FRESH FISH

In shopping for fresh fish use your three senses—sight, smell, and touch. It pays to be alert, without fear of looking firmly into a protruding eye. The best fish is still the *freshest* fish. It goes without saying that the freshest fish has superior flavor and texture, so learn to determine this optimum quality by checking fish closely for a number of signs, including the eye, which will be clear, the pupil black and protruding, if the fish is fresh.

The first sense that comes into play in selecting fish is the sense of smell. People who know their fish always put their nose to the flesh along the backbone, where it spoils first. If it smells like cucumber, or if it's odorless, the fish is fresh. In general, it may be said that a really fresh fish smells sweet and mild, with ocean fish having a subtle marine scent of endless waves. Fresh shark and skate have an ammonia smell, which disappears after a few days. A fishy odor is grounds for immediate rejection, since it means the fish has begun to decompose.

The sense of sight in determining freshness comes into play by examining the fish for color. Most fish, except for the salmon and trout family, have white meat with flesh that looks moist, almost translucent. If the flesh looks "muddy" or discolored around the edges, the fish is far from fresh. Some brook trout have yellow flesh; the color of salmon ranges from pink to orange. In a fresh fish the gills are usually reddish or pink. The scales should be bright, shiny, and closely adhering to the skin. The eyes must be bright, clear, and protruding.

It's not at all wrong to touch the fish. With your finger pressing firmly into the flesh you'll be able to tell a lot about its condition. A fish that's past its prime has dry meat that feels stiff to the touch. The flesh should be firm and elastic, and it should spring back when pressed.

At home, fish should be eaten immediately to savor its finest flavor and texture. If you're planning your shopping for three days or more, use the fish the first night to get the best of its quality. If fish is stored, put it in the coldest part of the refrigerator near the bottom either in a covered dish or loosely covered with plastic wrap, or wrapped in moisture-proof paper.

FROZEN FISH

When a particular fish is called for in a recipe of The Good Fat Diet and it's not available fresh, choose another appropriate fresh fish, or decide to settle for the less-than-perfect frozen alternative. In most cases, The Good Fat Diet allows frozen fish (if correctly thawed) to be substituted in recipes calling for the same fish in its fresh state. In that case, buying frozen fish requires as much alertness on your part as buying fresh fish.

Much can be predicted from merely looking at the frozen fish package. Fish spoils easily, so make sure the package is solidly frozen. Reject packages that have torn wrappings, misshapen boxes, or icy rims at the edges. There should be little or no air space in the packing, as this risks spoilage. Blood in a package means the fish has thawed and been refrozen, which makes it taste dry and dull, if it has not actually spoiled.

When you open the package, there should be no frost or ice crystals present, or any sign of white patches that indicate "freezer burn." The flesh should have a uniform glossy appearance; if it lacks the gloss while at the same time the surface looks "cottony" and releases liquid when pressed, it has probably been thawed and refrozen. Should you eat it in this condition—which I do not advise—you'll probably find that it has a strong "fishy," rancid taste.

──────────● AVOID "RUDE" ROOM TEMPERATURE ●──────────

If you've stored frozen fish in the freezer and wish to defrost it, try to avoid thawing at room temperature; though quicker, it causes loss of liquid, which is detrimental in terms of flavor, texture, and nutrients. A twenty-four–hour stay in the coldest part of the refrigerator is best for frozen fish to defrost.

For a quicker method that avoids the rude shock of room temperature, partially thaw the fish in the refrigerator, then wrap it in a plastic bag, seal well, and place it in a bowl of cold water until defrosting is completed. (Remember, breaded fish foods should never be thawed before cooking, because when fish thaws, it releases moisture, which seeps into the breading and makes it soggy.

If you don't fish yourself, you may find it economical to buy a large fresh fish, divide it into serving portions, freeze, and serve it over a period. Freezing is the best way of preserving the quality of fish. With proper care at each step of the procedure, fish will retain its flavor for many months.

The popular belief is that once fish is frozen, its quality is preserved. Actually, the true fact is that quite frequently fish is frozen improperly, a condition that can always be spotted by the flesh, dry and tough, and the taste—bad. When freezing fish, give consideration to both the type of protective package used and the proper storage temperature. It's useful sometimes to know the freezing properties of different species, so ask your fishman for special tips about freezing. Before freezing fish, follow these procedures:

• If the fish is to be stored longer than three months, leave it whole or in large pieces to reduce moisture loss.
• Make sure the fish is thoroughly cleaned, which means scaled and gutted with head and fin removed and the blood washed off. If

slime is a problem, rinse the fish in a solution of one teaspoon vinegar to three quarts cold water.

• Divide the cleaned fish into family-sized servings.

• Wrap the fish first with cling wrap or aluminum foil and then overwrap with freezer paper.

• Squeeze out as much air as possible from the package. Air pockets cause the flesh to dry out and turn rancid.

• Tape or tie the package securely. Label it with the date, the kind of fish, the number of servings, and the type of cut.

• Place the packages in the coldest part of the freezer (near the bottom). Roughly, two pounds of fish per cubic foot of space will freeze within twelve to twenty-four hours. Don't overload the freezer.

• Keep the freezer at 0°F or colder.

• Use fish frozen the longest first.

Packaging is important in freezing fish, since it provides barriers to spoiling agents, chiefly water vapor and oxygen. There is a great difference in the suitability of various wrapping materials:

• Aluminum foil and cling wraps cling well to surfaces and eliminate air pockets; they're excellent barriers to both water vapor and oxygen. A problem with aluminum foil, however, is that it's easily punctured.

• Freezer bags, usually made of polyester, are good barriers to water vapor and oxygen, but you may have a problem forcing out all the air from the package. Commercial packagers evacuate the air by vacuum pumping or heat shrinking.

• To force out much of the air of the freezer bag containing the fish, submerge it in water up to the top without letting the water flow in. Use the water pressure to force all the air out of the bag, then seal tightly.

• Freezer paper provides limited barriers to spoiling agents and serves best as an outer protective wrap over an inner wrap of aluminum foil or cling wrap.

• For freezing purposes, waxed paper, cartons, plastic freezer bags, or cellophane alone offer little protection.

Cooked fish should not be kept frozen for more than three months. Other than shrimp, crab, or lobster, freeze cooked fish only when it is in a sauce. With this exception, there are a number of practical and even ingenious ways to lengthen the freezer life of fish:

• Chiefly for lean freshwater fish, combine about five tablespoons of salt with two quarts of water to make a brine solution in which the fish is dipped for thirty seconds, then thoroughly wrap.

• For oily fish, like mackerel, freeze the fish in the brine solution in a container—a milk carton, metal loaf pan, or plastic container will do; then after briefly dipping the container in hot water, take out the block in which the fish is frozen, wrap the block in plastic or aluminum, seal, and return the package to the freezer.

• On a cookie sheet freeze the fish cut in its final cooking form and wrapped in plastic wrap. When solidly frozen take it off the sheet and immerse completely in ice water until a thin coat of ice has formed. Repeat this glazing process about three or four times, wrap, and store. The fish will keep about two months, after which the method must be reapplied.

9.

The Twenty-Minute Meal: Quick Ways to Prepare Fish

The reason many of us long missed out on the delights of preparing seafood at home is basically because we always felt somewhat daunted by the process known as fish preparation. Until they became converts to The Good Fat Diet program, many of our friends would order seafood in restaurants but did not often prepare fish at home. Characteristically, their knowledge concerning fish preparation for the most part confined itself to breading and frying it in oil, thereby killing all the flavor. The program I created, which is high in fish fat and low in calories, has helped them become fine fish cooks. They acquired this skill by following the recipes in The Good Fat Diet, designed especially to get the most flavor out of fish.

Often when connoisseurs sing the praises of this or that particular fish, they are in actuality paying tribute to a flavor that derives from the fat content of the fish. The salmon, lake trout or lake whitefish, herring, pompano, and Arctic char are high in fat, which contributes significantly to the distinct flavor of these fish. Fat generally is a great enhancer of taste, and in fish, where the flaky texture of meat is most desirable, it contributes to the density and size of the flake. In The Good Fat Diet it is no accident that the fish are tasty in and of themselves, because what qualifies them for the program is precisely their high content of fat, which, in addition, is good fat, since it contains large amounts of *Omega-3.*

GETTING FISH READY FOR COOKING

The fish bought in the market are generally already cleaned and dressed and need little further work to be made ready for cooking. Quite often, however, fish do need some additional work. When that happens, you may be called upon to perform the following operations:

• *Cleaning*—If all the scales have not been removed, use a knife, and beginning at the tail, working toward the head, draw the knife over the fish, especially on the flank, where the largest number of scales are found. To keep the scales from flying, incline the knife slightly toward you. Then with a cloth moistened with cold water wipe the fish thoroughly inside out, especially along the backbone, to remove any spots of clotted blood. If you perform this operation frequently, you may want to get a scaling knife; it has a rough-toothed surface that makes it easy to remove scales.

• *Skinning*—Cut off the fins along the back with a sharp knife; then cut a line formed by the removal of a narrow strip of skin along the entire length of back. From this line work the skin free around the bony part of the gills; the skin will strip off without trouble if the fish is fresh. Turn the fish and continue skinning on the other side. Soft flesh tears easily; in that case work slowly.

• *Boning*—A fish is "boned" for two reasons: either for stuffing it or the bones are troublesome. Fish need to be cleaned and skinned before boning. From the tail, run a sharp knife under the flesh along the entire length of backbone. Keep the knife close to the bone; cut clean and the flesh is easily removed from one side; then repeat the operation on the other side. Fish that are often boned are halibut, haddock, whitefish, and cod. Cooked whole fish that are often boned are roundfish, such as trout and pompano, and small sea bass. With a table knife these can be split in half, so the top half can be lifted aside, making it easy for the backbone to be lifted out.

COOKING FISH

The principles of cooking meat apply to cooking fish. Both use much the same methods and terminology, but since the prime ingredient is different, there are slight variations. Bear in mind that fish cooks faster than animal meats. Many cuts of meat require longer cooking because often they're tough and need more time to become tender. Fish, on the other hand, requires relatively brief cooking, since its meat is naturally tender and it contains much less fibrous tissue than meat. At the same time, pay greater attention to heat when cooking fish, since too much heat causes the flesh to shrink and become tough and ultimately flake apart.

● CANNED FISH? ●

Canned salmon, tuna, and sardines are a quick and convenient source of *Omega-3,* but beware! Some of these products may pose hazards to heart patients on low-salt diets. That's because some canning increases fat content as well as sodium levels. The same goes for most fast-food fish and prepared frozen-fish entrées.

In the case of canned tuna, it's best to choose water packed over oil packed. Nevertheless, in order to get rid of surplus salt, rinse under cold running water.

The great American gourmet James Beard, a great lover of fish cooking, said it well in defining the first principle of this art. "No matter what your choice in fish, remember this, all fish should be cooked quickly until it flakes easily when tested with a fork or toothpick." In line with Beard's dictum, here are the three essential "survival" points of cooking fish:

• Don't overcook. It destroys the flavor because cooking fish at too high a temperature toughens the meat and dries it out.
• A fish is ready for eating when the flesh changes from translucent to an opaque appearance, the point, in fact, when protein coagulates. Fork-test the fish for doneness in the thickest part of the flesh. When pierced with a fork, properly cooked fish flakes easily.
• Handle fish as little as possible during and after cooking, since fish flesh is tender and its appearance easily destroyed.

Note: If a recipe in The Good Fat Diet calls for a fresh fish and it's not available, you may substitute the same fish in its frozen state. Fillets must be defrosted and separated; otherwise frozen fish may be cooked without defrosting. For best results, however, the fish should be properly thawed, then patted dry before frying or broiling.

─────────────● THE CANADIAN COOKING METHOD ●─────────────

When a few years ago the Canadian Department of Fisheries released its results of experiments and tests on fish cooking times, one writer hailed it as "probably one of the most important announcements in fish cookery of the last century."

Whether or not it is may be disputed, but certainly the Canadian method is a simple and reliable way to determine when fish is done. The basic principle is to measure the fish at its thickest point and allow ten minutes of cooking time for every inch of thickness if the fish is fresh, twenty minutes for every inch if it is frozen. Thus a fresh fish measuring two and one-half inches would cook for twenty-five minutes.

The Canadian method applies to baking, broiling, braising, sautéing, frying, poaching, steaming—every sort of cooking; but because fish is so delicate, as well as by reason of other variables in cooking, the Canadian method should be modified by using the fork test for doneness. Press the fork inward into the thickest part of the flesh; the fish is done if the flesh is opaque and does not cling to the bones.

COOKING METHODS

The terms used in fish cookery are familiar. Yet in "terms" of The Good Fat Diet it may be well to define precisely what is meant by:

• *Poaching*—Cooking in a simmering liquid.
• *Steaming*—Cooking by steam generated from boiling water.
• *Baking*—Cooking by dry heat, usually in an oven.
• *Boiling*—Cooking in a liquid at a rolling boil.
• *Broiling*—Cooking by a dry heat method (this is intense heat, direct, from only one source).

• *Grilling*—Cooking over hot coals.

• *Stir-frying*—Cooking in a wok in a small amount of fat or oil.

Cooking methods *do* make a difference. Calories and cholesterol are added when fish is fried in butter or saturated fat. Breading or coating fish in butter or inundating it with hollandaise sauce similarly defeats the purpose of weight- and health-risk reduction. Heavy sauces are *out*; baking, broiling, and poaching fish, along with seasoning with wine, lemon juice, and herbs, are the most wholesome ways of keeping to The Good Fat Diet.

Perhaps the most popular way of cooking fish on The Good Fat Diet is by broiling fillets. It's the best alternative to frying. Any variety of fish may be prepared in this way, but trout, salmon, and halibut are particularly tasty when broiled in fillets. Let's take a closer look at some of the methods of cooking that are particularly good in bringing out the finest flavor in fish.

─────────────● TIMETABLE FOR COOKING FISH ●─────────────

COOKING METHOD	AMOUNT	COOKING TEMP.	COOKING TIME
Baking:			
Dressed	3 pounds	350°F	45–60 min.
Fillets or steaks	1 pound	350°F	12–15 min.
Broiling:			
Fillets or steaks	2 pounds		10–16 min. (turning once)
Charcoal Broiling:			
Pan dressed	3 pounds	Moderate	10–16 min. (turning once)
Fillets or steaks	1 pound	Moderate	7–12 min. (turning once)
Pan-Frying:			
Pan dressed	3 pounds	Moderate	8–10 min. (turning once)

COOKING METHOD	AMOUNT	COOKING TEMP.	COOKING TIME
Fillets or steaks	1 pound	Moderate	4–7 min. (turning once)
Poaching Fillets or steaks	1 pound	Simmer	5–10 min.
Steaming: Fillets or steaks	1½ pounds	Boil	5–10 min.

• BROILED FISH

To broil fillets, do the following:

- Wash and dry the fish.
- Lightly season each fillet with herbs and pepper.
- Lay the fillets on a sheet of foil to keep the oven from getting dirty.
- Place the fillets under the broiler for about ten minutes or less on each side.
- Baste lightly with vegetable oil or Decalorized Butter (see page 62 for the recipe) to keep the fillets from getting dry or sticking to the foil.

Note: Fillets are very delicate, so be careful when turning them over. Test for doneness when the fillet is well browned by flaking off a small piece. Due to variables in heat and fillet thickness, cooking times may vary.

Before broiling rinse the fish in cold running water and dry with a paper towel. The broiler should be preheated, and if the fish is placed on a rack, make sure the rack is well greased. It's important to remember that overcooking is the bane of fish flavor, and in broiling, this undesirable condition is usually indicated by a very brown appearance.

In order to prevent this from happening, cook about four inches from the heat if the broiler is on at maximum heat. It's best to cook at moderate heat until the flesh shows a light tanning and flakes off easily under the fork test. Some fish that particularly lend themselves to broiling are small whole fish, such as brook trout and smelts.

Some fish need not be turned, being merely split and broiled, such as scrod, mackerel, pompano, and bluefish. Salmon steaks, halibut steaks, and fillets of fish are turned only if they are of considerable thickness. There's no need to turn thin pieces. Two pancake turners or two broad spatulas will help you move the fish without breaking it.

• DECALORIZED BUTTER

¼ pound sweet unsalted butter
¾ cup buttermilk

Leave the butter and the buttermilk at room temperature to soften the butter and remove the chill from the buttermilk. Place the butter in a 4-cup measure or small deep bowl. Whip with an electric hand mixer and slowly add the buttermilk. When the butter will not absorb any more buttermilk, pour off the remainder. This process increases the volume of butter by at least three times. Store in a crock and cover. Keep refrigerated.

Makes approximately 2 cups.

10 CALORIES PER TEASPOON.
35 CALORIES PER TABLESPOON.

• POACHED FISH

The timing for poaching fish, whether in water or any of the court bouillons, is exactly the same. First bring the water to the boiling point; then put the fish in it. Begin timing the fish when the water returns to the boiling point. Use the Canadian method for measuring cooking times, that is, ten minutes cooking per inch thickness for fresh fish, double that for frozen fish.

If the fish is cooked in court bouillon, make sure the liquid does not boil or bubble after placing the fish in it. Save the broth for sauces and as fish stock. After they are cooked, do not leave the fish in the bouillon, or they will taste tough and overdone. If the fish is left to cool in the bouillon, reduce the cooking time so the fish won't be overcooked.

The liquids used in poaching go by the various terms for broths that are closely connected with this delicious and low-calorie way of cooking fish. The three chief types of broths are:

• *Court bouillon*—Generally the word bouillon (French *boillir,* to boil) applies to any liquid in which vegetables, meat, or fish have been cooked, so all bouillons are broths. The court bouillon, however, is a liquid in which fish (or shellfish) have been cooked. The liquid commonly used is water, usually flavored with condiments, herbs, and aromatic vegetables that complement the fish. Red or white wine is also used to flavor the court bouillon.

• *Fish stock*—In contrast to court bouillon, fish stock is thicker and often looks gelatinous. That's because it's a concentrated broth made from bones, skins, heads, and other fish trimmings, which is used as the base of fish sauces, or to moisten fish in braising. Water and wine, generally in equal quantities, or sometimes wine alone, form the liquid to which bay leaf, onion, parsley, and other aromatics are usually added.

• *Fumet*—This is short for the French *fumet de poisson,* which is a fish stock that has been boiled down, that is, reduced in volume through evaporation, giving the stock a thicker consistency. The *fumet* is used chiefly as a base for sauces to go with fish. Since its essence is the concentrated liquid, a *fumet* can evolve from reduction of the court bouillon in which the fish has been poached. Further reduction of the *fumet* enables it to serve as a sauce on its own with different fish dishes.

• FRYING FISH

Frying fish is an extremely tasty way to prepare fish, but this process should be avoided if you're on the rapid-weight-loss program of The Good Fat Diet. Once you have shed the desired number of pounds, and you're ready to return to the balanced eating of The Good Fat Diet maintenance program (which should include two to three fish dishes a week), remember to fry fish only in the right oils. Most people believe that frying fish involves no more than putting some grease in the pan, turning up the heat, and tossing in the fillets. Keep in mind the following fish-frying rules to make the job easier and the fish tastier:

• Fry in vegetable oil or a vegetable oil/butter mixture. Blue smoke means you're using an oil too high in fat.

• Use the proper temperature. Fish fried too hot will show an outside that's brown and an inside that's raw. If the temperature is too low, the fish will be greasy and soggy, and you will have indigestion.

• Do not coat fillets with flour or cornmeal or other ingredients until they are ready for cooking. Otherwise, moisture from the fish will be absorbed by the coating, which results in fried fish that is neither brown nor crisp to the degree it should be.

● WINES WITH FISH ●

Wine has been long noted as an excellent companion to fish. Heart researchers have discovered that moderate alcohol consumption also results in lowering the body's LDL (bad cholesterol) levels and raises HDL's (the good cholesterol).

Gourmets frown on red wine with fish dishes because it tends to overpower the delicate flavor of fish. However, on The Good Fat Diet you will find that a rosé or a young light-bodied red wine goes very well with the rich-tasting fish favored for their high *Omega-3* contents, such as salmon or tuna. Similarly, a robust red wine can be delightful with a Mediterranean-type fish stew that includes tomatoes, garlic, and herbs.

Most fish have a slight sweetness, however, which is best complemented by a dry white wine served well chilled. The light acidity of this wine is especially well suited to the rich flavors associated in French cooking with poached white fish. In this category belong French white wines from the Rhone Valley (Muscadet, Hermitage), Italian wines (Soave, Frascati), and a dry Chardonnay or Fumé Blanc from California.

It's been suggested for fish of finer quality, sole or turbot, for instance, to choose a "rounder flavor" of one of the better white burgundies. These include the French Grand Cru Chablis, the dry-delicate German Moselle wines, and, from California, the Chenin Blanc.

Instead of a dry wine some people like to eat their fish with the accompaniment of a fruity wine, with its slightly sweeter savor. A Riesling from California would do admirably for this purpose, as would a Gewurztraminer from Alsace, or a German Auslese.

• STIR-FRYING (OR DIETING WITH A WOK)

Stir-frying has become America's favorite way to eat seafood, thanks to the phenomenal popularity of Chinese-style seafood restaurants. Healthful stir-frying means cooking in a wok using a small amount of unsaturated oil. This technique evolved by the Chinese, and diffused throughout Asia, has in the past ten years become very popular with Americans who have discovered that using the wok means a calorie-conscious way of cooking that's at the same time delicious and quick.

In stir-frying, the cooking time is extremely short. Therefore, it's important to prepare everything in advance of cooking. Stir-fried dishes should always be cooked just before serving, since they do not bear up very well under reheating.

It is one of the principles of stir-frying that the items are cut according to the designated shape and size called for by the recipe. This usually means a shape that's in conformity with the main component of the dish. For example, if noodles are the principal ingredient, then cut anything added to the dish in the way of vegetables or other ingredients into thin strips matching the shape of the noodles. Make sure to wash and drain ingredients thoroughly because the cooking process is harmed by excess water, which lowers the temperature of the oil. Place all ingredients within easy reach of the stove, preferably in the order of their addition to the pan for cooking.

Next, heat up the wok over a high flame; then put in a small amount of oil and swirl it around to coat the pan. Drop in the ingredients, followed by the seasonings, and constantly stir and toss the ingredients in the wok. Continue this quick frenzy for at most a few minutes. By cooking with a wok over an intense heat, the actual cooking process may take as little as ten seconds or less.

———● STIR-FRYING FISH: THE CHINESE TWO-STEP METHOD ●———

Virtually every Chinese restaurant uses the two-step method in preparing stir-fried dishes. The two-step method helps preserve especially the delicate texture of seafood and fish, which may be bruised or torn in the rough-and-tumble of stir-fried cooking.

The first step involves coating the seafood with cornstarch and seasonings. This is then cooked in part in a thin film of medium-hot oil. The oil gives the seafood a smooth, velvety texture that effectively seals in the juices.

The second step completes the cooking process. Return the fried fish to the pan and toss with the other ingredients, which have been already cooked in the wok.

• STEAMING FISH

There are many fish connoisseurs who believe there's no better way to bring out the flavor of seafood than steaming. It's generally agreed to be an excellent way to keep the flesh moist and tender, with its flavor intact. Steaming fish retains the natural juices, which are frequently lost during other cooking methods.

Steaming fish requires a shallow dish or plate containing the ingredients. This is then set uncovered on a "platform" or rack inside a deep pot. The "platform" might be a wok or cake rack, or any other object that raises the shallow dish about two inches above the water in the pot. The dish is elevated so that when the water boils beneath it, no splashes will fall into the ingredients contained in the dish. While the water boils, the lid in the pot should remain tightly closed.

If you plan to do a lot of fish steaming, it's handy to have a set of steamers, such as the aluminum sets that are popular or the bamboo steamers that look like decorative baskets. In steaming fish it's important to maintain an even flow of steam; so keep the heat on high throughout the cooking process. For longer steaming, the boiling water may occasionally have to be replenished in order to ensure that there will be enough steam to cook the food. Remember, after turning off the heat don't leave the fish too long in the pot, as residual heat will continue to overcook them. Fish should be served the moment it comes off the stove.

THE GOOD FAT KITCHEN

By stocking your kitchen with the items listed below, you'll be fully prepared to follow The *Good Fat* Diet's fourteen-day rapid-weight-loss program.

Utensils
Cheesecloth
Garlic press
Small scale
Nonstick frying pans (small, medium, and large)
Wok (optional)

Dairy
Nonfat milk
Cultured nonfat buttermilk powder
Nonfat buttermilk
Nonfat yogurt

Pasta
Whole-wheat spaghetti
Whole-wheat macaroni

Breads
Whole-wheat bread
Corn tortillas
Whole-wheat pita bread

Rice
Brown rice
Long-grain rice

Beans
Black beans
Kidney beans
Pinto beans
Garbanzo beans

Vegetables
Green bell peppers
Red bell peppers
Onions
Tomatoes
Romaine lettuce
Radishes
Celery
Carrots
Zucchini
Sweet potatoes
Yellow squash
Turnips
Rutabagas
Asparagus
Beets
Cucumbers

Chives
Alfalfa sprouts
Bean sprouts (will spoil if not used
   in 2–3 days)
Mushrooms
Squash (crooked, butternut, acorn)
Cabbage
Green peas
Eggplant
Parsley
Potatoes
Watercress
Fresh ginger
Fresh garlic
Spinach

Spices

Oregano	Cayenne pepper
Basil (fresh or dried)	Cinnamon
Thyme	Cloves
Marjoram	Coriander
Rosemary	Curry powder
Bay leaves	Ground cumin
Anise	Dill weed
Dill seed	Horseradish
Dry mustard	Mace
White vinegar	Nutmeg
Low-salt soy sauce	Paprika
Fresh garlic	Chili powder (without salt)
Ginger powder	Cardamom
Yeast	Parsley
Bouillon (beef or chicken)	Pepper (white/black)

10.

Our Troubled Food Chain: How Safe Is Fish?

When we decided to implement our new dietary program, it was not until after I educated myself on one very important question. Because much of our environment suffers from chemical pollution, the same question must rightly be asked of every item we eat. In view of the widespread publicity concerning contamination of the seas, I wanted to know the extent to which chemical pollutants affect the waters in which fish live.

My investigation of this topic put me once again on familiar biochemical ground. I was also fortunate in that the issue of chemical pollution has lately become one of the most voluminously documented areas of science. There are many reasons why many chemical residues, especially pesticides and PCBs (polychlorinated biphenyls), are worrisome. But at the end of my investigation I was satisfied that it is as safe to eat fish as it is to eat bread, tomatoes, chicken, or any of the rest of the fruits of earth and sea, all of which are subject to the same chemical assault by man on his environment.

The outpouring of chemical substances into the air, earth, and water is the unfortunate result of our way of life. The vast complex of industrial and power plants, along with the massive amount of car exhausts, contribute to our pollution problem. Like all edible things, fish are not immune to this chemical onslaught. Fish farthest out in the deep sea are apparently least affected by man's chemical inundation of the environment, but luckily scientists have found that even fish exposed to contaminants may have negligible levels of chemicals in the edible flesh. At any rate, it's useful to know which fish are most exposed and how to avoid eating those parts of the fish that are contaminated.

The chief villains here are pesticides and PCBs. Some people are concerned about acid rain, which consists of two acids, sulfuric acid from coal-burning power plants and nitric acid from car exhausts that condense in clouds and are returned to the earth through rain or snow. Acid rain destroys the ecosystem, forests, and crops, but it does not affect us as fish eaters because once a lake becomes too acidic, it kills the fish before they can reach our table.

Pesticides are more troublesome both because they are longer lived and are absorbed by the prime food of marine life, phytoplankton. These chemical substances resist breakdown, resulting in the accumulation of the substances in the environment, and their entry into the bottom of the food chain through phytoplankton means that, as they are passed along the chain, these chemical substances may harm the organisms living there, eventually affecting man. What's more, each link in the food chain concentrates the chemicals, so the pollutants in the organisms of an ecosystem increase drastically as the pollutants move up the food chain.

Even more worrisome than pesticides are PCBs. These synthetic compounds, formerly used industrially, are now banned from production. PCBs are extremely difficult to destroy; they are resistant to degradation, highly toxic, and believed to be carcinogenic. They can enter the skin and gills of fish, so these fish may incorporate chemical substances other than by eating organisms in the food chain.

Some chemical substances can be absorbed by fish but are not easily secreted. They usually accumulate in organs like the liver, which we do not usually consume, and in fatty tissues.

Among the fish species, some are more likely than others to have high concentrations of PCBs. This depends mostly on the location that exposes them to PCB contamination. Only a few fish are believed to have high levels, and these must be seen in terms of geographical location. In New Jersey, for instance, the site of many industrial complexes, the species found to have been principally affected are striped bass, American eel, bluefish, white perch, and white catfish. These should be avoided to minimize exposure to PCBs in seafood. On the whole, freshwater fish are more likely to have higher levels of PCBs than marine ones.

Aware of the dangers of the chemical substances dumped into our waters by industries and power plants, a number of government agencies have stepped in to prevent fish exposed to PCBs from reaching the American dining table. The chief way to prevent this from happening has been an effort to remove from the marketplace such fish that contains PCB levels above the regulatory action level set by the Food and Drug Administration. Several states monitor a variety of fish from their waters, imposing strict fishing limits should PCBs exceed the limits of the legal tolerance of 2 ppm (parts per million). The risk of eating PCB-exposed fish is gradually growing less, as many cities and states are giving higher priority to cleaning up local waterways. In fact, some East Coast rivers are seeing the return of salmon that pollutants had once driven away. The pesticide DDT and the industrial chemical PCB, the most dangerous pollutants, have been banned by legislation.

Though PCBs are the most harmful of the chemicals to be found in some waters, it is believed that there are not many fish with very high levels. It is, nevertheless, advisable not to eat those parts of the fish likely to have PCB concentrations. Since PCBs are accumulated in fatty tissues, it is possible to trim those portions, that is, the dark meat, the skin and exterior fat, and belly fat. The risk of eating a certain amount of PCBs is further reduced if the fish is boiled or baked, rather than fried.

It is also obvious that the chance of consuming fish products high in contamination is minimized by eating a wide variety of seafoods rather than varieties that are known to have high PCB levels.

● AVOID PCBs ●

Not many fish may be high in PCBs, but it is desirable to avoid those that are. People who consume a great deal of fish from contaminated waters, such as some sports fish from the Great Lakes or certain species from eastern coastal waters, need to be especially alerted to the PCB hazard. Pregnant and nursing women are another group that should take extra caution in avoiding PCB contaminated fish, since these chemicals pose possible risk to nursing infants. Women of child-bearing age generally should be aware that among the adverse effects of PCBs are reproductive disorders.

BEWARE OF TOXINS

Another toxic element to which fish may be exposed comprises certain metals, primarily mercury, lead, cadmium, and arsenic. This process, known as "heavy metal contamination," has become widely publicized through the attention given to mercury and its role in the so-called Minamata disease, studied in Japan and Canada. The fish usually affected by this contamination are the freshwater species found in the rivers and lakes where mercury wastes are dumped by industrial plants. Like pesticides and PCBs, mercury also is absorbed at the bottom of the food chain through phytoplankton.

A report on people eating fish with comparatively high levels of mercury, including children and women of child-bearing age, found that even these unsafe levels did not constitute a hazard. The FDA regularly monitors mercury in certain fish, including swordfish, as well as some other species associated with high mercury, such as Pacific halibut, tuna, shark, and king mackerel. A recent study from the National Marine Fisheries Service in Washington, D.C., on people eating fish with high mercury levels concluded that "mercury in seafood poses little hazard to the seafood-eating public." Of the other metals, the significant element is arsenic, of which seafood is a chief dietary source; meat and poultries contain smaller amounts. Arsenic is contained in pesticides sprayed on food crops and in animal food additives. Its entry into the food chain has of late slowed down; since the late sixties farmers have begun using less arsenic-containing pesticides.

Despite such possible threats, the increase of two to three fish-centered meals a week as recommended by The Good Fat Diet should not raise any qualms in the consumer. Government control and public awareness are powerful agencies in keeping fish species suspected of contamination from the marketplace. And the benefit of *Omega-3*, with its powerful effect on atherosclerosis, which leads to heart disease, the nation's number one killer, outweighs by far any danger posed by chemical contamination.

11.

The Good Fat Kitchen— Making It Work

In going from a meat- to a fish-centered diet, the most important step concerns the recipes. Thus far we've looked at the science of *Omega-3* and the theory behind good fat cooking. Now you are actually going to enter The Good Fat Kitchen.

It's a truism that if people are to shed weight rapidly and maintain their new figures, they must enjoy what they eat. Ultimately, if their diet is to be a success and remain a permanent part of their lives, they must learn to prepare dishes that are as good as or better than the ones they're replacing. That's why The Good Fat Diet menus follow three standards: the recipes must be simple, practical, and—above all—tasty.

Once you have mastered the simple cooking elements, you will be astonished that fish can be so delicious. The Good Fat Diet recipes incorporate imaginative new ways of preparing dishes designed to make you forget there ever was such a thing as red meat. The Good Fat Kitchen is meant to encourage a new way of cooking in order to change familiar but unhealthy eating patterns. As such, it is as much a learning experience as it is a prescription for weight loss and health.

While following the fish-centered program of The Good Fat Diet, you will obtain a flair for substituting low-calorie ingredients for fats, oils, and sugars. These substitutions are calculated to please the palate. You will learn to make dishes low in animal fats and discover the zesty flavors that fish imparts to meals. And you will be surprised to see how fast your high-fat eating habits become ancient history.

Thus, innovative ideas on spicing, creative methods of mixing, and all kinds of delicious combinations will become part of your dazzling new cooking techniques. At the same time, however, you will be absorbing the discipline vital to making The Good Fat Kitchen a permanent fixture.

By using the shopping information, you become accustomed to allocating your resources. By following the recipes, you automatically learn to diminish fats and oils in your cooking. By being encouraged to think creatively, you discover new ways of making vegetables and grains taste delicious. The recipes teach you the planning so necessary to rational eating.

If you follow The Good Fat Diet menus, meal-planning becomes a natural part of your daily routine. Thus, you think of salads and soups in addition to the entrée. For the entrée your first thoughts will be how to reduce high-fat components. You'll think of new flavoring agents to mix with fish, rice, vegetables, stews, casseroles, and salads. And once you've attained this point in meal planning, you will have come a long way in modifying your eating behavior.

The Good Fat Kitchen is full of surprises, and not long after adopting the program you will continually discover new ideas for the preparation of dishes. That's when your food consumption pattern will have permanently changed for the better.

Before you enter on your new adventure in cooking, remember that your dishes will be tastier and more nutritious if you use fresh and unprocessed ingredients. While it's true that many of these recipes can be prepared from canned or frozen goods, always try to get fresh items. Whenever possible, use the whole grains instead of refined ones. The taste and texture of whole grains are better for you.

A WORD ABOUT WEIGHT LOSS

Now that you know what *Omega-3* is and the benefits it contains for your health, you will be pleased to learn how The Good Fat Diet can help shed unwanted body fat. To most people there's something unnerving about the weight-loss process. The word "diet" conjures up to them a forbidding regimen that spells trial and ordeal. But The Good Fat Diet holds none of these terrors. If you abide by a few simple rules, you will find no difficulty in losing as much as ten pounds in two weeks in the safest and most efficient manner possible.

What makes The Good Fat Diet program different is the special care with which the menus have been selected. They have been particularly chosen to make rapid weight loss a delight to the palate and a filling satisfaction to the stomach. In fact, The Good Fat Diet program is unlike any other diet in that, with a few slight changes or additions for nondieters, it provides an eating program rich in *Omega-3* that the whole family can enjoy. So while you're "dieting," other members of the family will benefit from the sound nutrition you are giving them in their less strictly constituted portions of the same meal.

It should be additionally gratifying to know that with The Good Fat Diet you're putting yourself back in balance with the way man was intended to eat. The program provides you with natural vitamins so often missing from the typical American diet of processed foods and refined grains.

As you eat more fish, you'll also learn to eat more vegetables, whole grains, and citrus fruits. The Good Fat Diet shows you that vegetables need not taste like "rabbit food." If you're on a weight-loss program, try to adopt these dietary patterns:

• Have a plastic sandwich bag with raw vegetables and a piece of fresh fruit handy when you go out and don't expect to have a meal soon. That way you'll never get too hungry.

• In spicing and seasoning, go by taste preference rather than the recipe instructions.

• Eat more whole-grain foods and beans.

• Eat fresh fruits, preferably citrus fruits and apples, instead of sugary snacks.

• Once you've lost weight and obtained a stable weight level, keep a careful eye on fats and calories. The Good Fat Diet maintenance program makes controlling your new weight level easier than ever before.

• Drink plenty of water—six to eight glasses a day. Beware of fruit juices and sodas, which are usually no more than sugar suspended in colored water.

12.

The Fourteen-Day Good Fat Diet Program: A Scientific Way to Rapid Weight Loss

BEVERAGES

Drink plenty of water while you're on The Good Fat Diet rapid-weight-loss program. Water is good for you at all times, but many of us do not always welcome it with our meals, preferring a cup of coffee or a glass of wine instead. Though moderation is the key word here, a cup of coffee or a glass of wine (approximately 100 calories) every day or every other day with your meal will not substantially alter the beneficial weight-loss effects of The Good Fat Diet.

Greater caution must be taken for fruit juices. It's a common fault of dieters to believe that they can drink juices without adding on weight. Fruit juices, however, contain many hidden calories that add up rapidly and interfere with The Good Fat Diet rapid-weight-loss program.

BREAKFAST

Though *Omega-3* meets the vital health needs by replacing bad with good fat, it does not address the important need for fiber. Naturally, there's fiber in many of the recipes in The Good Fat Diet program, but in order to ensure that you do get adequate amounts of this component, we recommend that you get your fiber intake at a time we found to be most suitable, that is, in the morning with breakfast in the form of cereal.

No matter whether you're losing weight rapidly or wish to maintain it at its desired level, don't forget to start your day with a necessary breakfast of a half cup of cereal containing fiber with a half cup of fresh fruit, if you like. By doing so, you'll meet two necessary requirements of good dieting: You'll be having a nourishing breakfast and you'll be consuming more fiber. Please use the following chart in designing the breakfast most desirable to your tastes, or use the four sample breakfast plans we provided for guidelines.

●——— FIBER CONTENT OF SELECTED BREADS, CEREALS, AND FRUITS ●———

BREADS AND CEREALS	FIBER (grams per ounce)	CALORIES
Fiber One	12	60
100% Bran	9	90
All-Bran	9	70
Bran Buds	8	90
Corn Bran	5	120
Bran Chex	4.4	100
Fruitful Bran	4	120
Raisin Bran	4	120
40% Bran Flakes	4	90
Wheatena	4	120
Wheaties	4	110
Shredded Wheat	3.5	90
Grape-Nuts	3	100
Corn Flakes	3	110
Oatmeal, uncooked (⅓ cup)	1.9	110
Whole-wheat bread (1 slice)	2.1	70
Rye bread (1 slice)	1.2	65

FRUITS	FIBER (grams per ounce)	CALORIES
Apple, 1		
3 in.	3.3	70
Applesauce		
½ cup	2.6	50
Apricots, dried		
¼ cup	7.8	100
Banana, sliced		
½ cup	2.6	50
Nectarine, 1		
medium	3	35
Orange, 1		
2½ in.	2.4	65
Peach, 1		
2½ in.	1.4	35
Pear, 1		
2½ in.	2.6	100
Raspberries		
½ cup	4.6	35
Strawberries		
½ cup	1.7	26

• BREAKFAST 1

1 slice dry toast
½ grapefruit
½ cup bran cereal
1 cup nonfat milk
black coffee or tea

300 CALORIES.

• **BREAKFAST 2**

½ cup apple juice
⅔ cup carbonated water (combine with apple juice)
1 orange
1 slice dry toast
½ banana
black coffee or tea

240 CALORIES.

• **BREAKFAST 3**

½ cantaloupe, 5-inch diameter
½ cup cereal
1 cup nonfat milk
½ small banana, thinly sliced
black coffee or tea

235 CALORIES.

• **BREAKFAST 4**

1 small banana
1 cup nonfat milk
½ teaspoon ground cinnamon
⅛ teaspoon ground nutmeg
(Combine all ingredients in blender and serve over crushed ice.)

½ toasted bagel
½ ounce cheddar cheese
black coffee or tea

253 CALORIES.

DAY 1

Breakfast:
Breakfast 1

Lunch:
Raw Vegetable Antipasto
½ cup Eggplant Dip
1 apple or 1 orange

Dinner:
Tomato Soup
Cajun-Style Salmon
Sautéed Shredded Cabbage 'n' Mushrooms
½ cup steamed rice
1 apple or 1 orange

1,135 CALORIES PER DAY.

DAY 2

Breakfast:
Breakfast 3

Lunch:
Rainbow Fruit Salad
Blueberry Bran Muffin

Dinner:
Marinated Grilled Chicken Breast
Glazed Cauliflower
Green Salad with Italian Dressing
1 baked potato
1 tablespoon margarine or 2 tablespoons Decalorized Butter
½ cup apple juice

1,157 CALORIES PER DAY.

DAY 3

─────────────────────●─────────────────────

Breakfast:
Breakfast 2

Lunch:
Salmon Pasta Salad
½ cup Nonfat Yogurt
Celery and carrot sticks

Dinner:
Vichyssoise
Poached Salmon Steak with Dill Sauce
Italian Rice

1,153 CALORIES PER DAY.

DAY 4

─────────────────────●─────────────────────

Breakfast:
Breakfast 1

Lunch:
Four-Bean Salad
1 pita bread
1 fruit (apple, pear, or orange)

Dinner:
Tandoori Chicken
Rice Pilaf
1 whole-wheat pita
Broccoli and Bean Sprouts Sauté
1 apple

1,154 CALORIES PER DAY.

DAY 5

Breakfast:
Breakfast 4

Lunch:
Gazpacho
Rice Salad Niçoise
½ cup strawberries, sliced, and ½ cup banana, sliced, combined

Dinner:
Veal in Mushroom and Tomato Sauce
Stuffed Potatoes
Italian Vegetable Stir-Fry

1,138 CALORIES PER DAY.

DAY 6

Breakfast:
Breakfast 3

Lunch:
Tossed Shredded Chicken Salad
Raw vegetables (celery, cauliflower, and zucchini)
1 fruit (apple, nectarine, or orange)

Dinner:
Steamed Fish, Chinese-Style
Fried Rice
1 fruit (½ cup banana, sliced, or ½ cup applesauce)

1,291 CALORIES PER DAY.

Day 7

Breakfast:
Breakfast 1

Lunch:
1 whole-wheat pita bread
Cucumbers in Yogurt
Fresh Orange Fruit Cups

Dinner:
Pasta Primavera
Asparagus with Lemon-Parsley Sauce
1 slice Garlic Bread
½ cup banana, sliced, or ½ cup apple, sliced

1,015 Calories per Day.

Day 8

Breakfast:
Breakfast 4

Lunch:
Chicken Relleno
2 Corn Tortillas
1 fruit (apple, orange, or pear)

Dinner:
Skewered Swordfish
Rice with Green Peppers and Mushrooms
Italian Vegetable Stir-Fry
Strawberry-Raspberry Soup

1,153 Calories per Day.

DAY 9

Breakfast:
Breakfast 2

Lunch:
Alaska-Style Cobb Salad
1 whole-wheat pita
Baked Apple Crunch

Dinner:
New Orleans Seafood Stew
Rice and Mushrooms
Pumpkin Pie

1,257 CALORIES PER DAY.

DAY 10

Breakfast:
Breakfast 3

Lunch:
Chicken in Pita Bread
Raw vegetables (celery and carrots)
¼ cup Creamy Orange-Peanut Dip

Dinner:
Seafood Kabobs
Eggplant over Pasta
1 slice Garlic Bread
Strawberry Ice

1,140 CALORIES PER DAY.

DAY 11

Breakfast:
Breakfast 1

Lunch:
Tabouli Salad
1 pita bread
1 fruit (apple, orange, or pear)

Dinner:
Eggplant Parmigiana (over ¼ pound pasta, such as spaghetti or macaroni)
Broiled Tomato Parmesan
2 slices Garlic Bread
Green Salad with Italian Dressing

1,180 CALORIES PER DAY.

DAY 12

Breakfast:
Breakfast 4

Lunch:
Clam Chowder
2 Bran Muffins
1 fruit (apple, orange, peach)

Dinner:
Broccoli Soup
Broiled Herbed Chicken
Sautéed Zucchini and Carrots
1 cup rice (brown or white)
1 cup strawberries

1,188 CALORIES PER DAY.

DAY 13

Breakfast:
Breakfast 1

Lunch:
Vegetable Soup
Szechuan Salad
½ cup steamed rice (white or brown)

Dinner:
Egg Foo Young
½ cup steamed rice (white or brown)
Fruit Cup

1,160 CALORIES PER DAY.

DAY 14

Breakfast:
Breakfast 4

Lunch:
String Bean Tuna Salad
1 fruit (½ cup strawberries, fresh or frozen; orange; or ½ cup sliced banana)
1 pita bread, or 1 slice whole-wheat bread

Dinner:
Chicken Tostada
Spanish Brown Rice
1 fruit (apple, or ½ cup raspberries, fresh or frozen)

1,133 CALORIES PER DAY.

13.

The Fourteen-Day Good Fat Diet Program: Recipes

DAY 1

⚫

• RAW VEGETABLE ANTIPASTO

4 mushrooms, thinly sliced
4 cherry tomatoes, thinly sliced
1 medium zucchini, cut julienne style
2 asparagus tips, chopped
½ cup broccoli, flowerets
4 radishes, thinly sliced
½ cucumber, cut into slices or sticks
1 carrot, shredded
½ cup cauliflower, flowerets
½ cup string beans, chopped
½ cup celery, cut into sticks

Use fresh vegetables, which are nutritious and high in energy, and which because of their content of complex carbohydrates are more easily metabolized. This is an appetizing antipasto that is not only tasty but easily transportable. Serve with the Eggplant Dip (recipe follows).

SERVES 4.
25 CALORIES PER SERVING.

• EGGPLANT DIP

1 medium eggplant
2 medium tomatoes, finely diced
4 tablespoons fresh parsley, finely chopped
1 clove garlic, crushed
¼ cup lemon juice (juice of 2 freshly squeezed lemons)
1 small onion, finely diced
1 teaspoon red chili powder
1 teaspoon cumin
½ teaspoon pepper, freshly ground

Preheat the oven to 350°F. Bake the whole eggplant in the oven approximately 45 to 60 minutes, or until it is soft. Allow it to cool; then peel and cube.

Add the eggplant and half of the diced tomatoes to a blender. Blend until smooth. Add the remaining ingredients to the eggplant puree and blend thoroughly. Pour into a serving dish. Chill for at least 1 hour.

Note: For a spicier dip add cayenne pepper and/or crushed garlic to taste.

MAKES 1½ CUPS.
30 CALORIES PER TABLESPOON.

• TOMATO SOUP

2 pounds ripe plum tomatoes (may substitute canned whole Italian plum
tomatoes)
3 shallots, peeled and chopped
⅓ cup fresh parsley, finely chopped
1 tablespoon bottled Italian seasoning (may substitute a combination of basil,
oregano, and rosemary)
2 cups water
4 teaspoons Parmesan cheese, grated
dried or fresh basil (for garnish)

Use firm, ripe, red tomatoes. Drop the tomatoes, one or two at a
time, in boiling water to cover, and boil for exactly 10 seconds.
Remove. Cut out the stems. Peel off the skin starting from the stem
holes (optional). Cut the tomatoes in half crosswise, not through the
stems. Squeeze each half gently to extract the seeds and juice from the
center of the tomato.

Add the shallots to the tomatoes and place in a blender; blend for
a few seconds to make a smooth puree. Put puree, parsley, Italian
seasoning, and water into a saucepan. Cover and cook over medium
heat for 10 minutes, then simmer for 20 minutes. Sprinkle 1 teaspoon
of grated Parmesan cheese over each serving, with a generous pinch
of dried or fresh basil.

SERVES 4.
40 CALORIES PER SERVING.

• CAJUN-STYLE SALMON

1 tablespoon olive oil
1 cup onion, finely diced
1 cup celery, finely diced
1 cup green pepper, finely diced
2 cloves garlic, crushed
2 cups fresh tomatoes, chopped
1½ cups chicken stock
½ teaspoon thyme
½ teaspoon chili powder
½ teaspoon salt
¼ teaspoon pepper, freshly ground
1 cup long-grain rice
1½ cups cooked fresh salmon, flaked

Place a large skillet over medium heat. Add olive oil. When the oil is hot, add the onion, celery, green pepper, and garlic. Sauté until the onion is soft. Add tomatoes, stock, thyme, chili powder, salt, and pepper. Bring to a boil and stir in the rice. Reduce heat, cover, and simmer slowly 17 minutes, stirring occasionally. Add salmon and cook 5 minutes, or until heated through. Place over the rice on a platter and serve.

SERVES 4.
350 CALORIES PER SERVING.

• SAUTÉED SHREDDED CABBAGE 'N' MUSHROOMS

2 pounds green cabbage
2 tablespoons olive oil
1 cup mushrooms, thinly sliced
1 teaspoon thyme
⅓ cup fresh parsley, finely chopped
½ teaspoon salt
¼ teaspoon pepper, freshly ground

Boil 2 quarts of water. Rinse the cabbage, cut it in half, cut away the core, then finely shred. Add the shredded cabbage to the boiling water, boiling for approximately 3 to 4 minutes. Immediately remove and place in a colander; rinse the cabbage in cold water to stop the cooking process.

Heat the olive oil in a large frying pan. Add and sauté the mushrooms until lightly browned. Sprinkle the thyme over the mushrooms, turning occasionally. Add the cabbage, parsley, salt, and pepper. Increase the heat to high and toss all the ingredients until the cabbage becomes limp, or slightly translucent.

SERVES 4.
65 CALORIES PER SERVING.

DAY 2

• RAINBOW FRUIT SALAD

1 cup fresh pineapple, cubed (or canned water-packed pineapple, drained, if not available fresh)
2 cups fresh oranges, cubed
1 cup (20) seedless grapes (any variety) (may substitute 20 blueberries or 20 raspberries)
1 ripe kiwi, peeled
2 teaspoons lime juice (or lemon juice)
2 tablespoons flaked coconut (optional)

Place the pineapple, oranges, and grapes in a large bowl. Puree the kiwi and lime juice in a blender. Pour the kiwi puree over the fruit and toss gently. Transfer the fruit to an airtight container and refrigerate. To serve, sprinkle flaked coconut on top of each portion.

SERVES 4.
82 CALORIES PER SERVING.

• BLUEBERRY BRAN MUFFINS

2 cups raw bran
1 cup rolled oats (oatmeal)
¼ cup whole-wheat flour
2 teaspoons cinnamon
1 teaspoon nutmeg
2 eggs, beaten
1 cup buttermilk
¼ cup molasses
2 cups fresh blueberries (or frozen blueberries, drained)

Preheat the oven to 350°F. Combine the bran, oats, flour, cinnamon, and nutmeg in a large mixing bowl. In a separate bowl combine the eggs, buttermilk, and molasses. Add to the bran mixture and mix lightly. Add the blueberries, again mixing lightly. Spoon the mixture into nonstick muffin tins. Bake for 40 minutes or until brown.

MAKES 24 MUFFINS.
60 CALORIES PER MUFFIN.

• MARINATED GRILLED CHICKEN BREASTS

4 chicken breasts, skin and fat removed
½ cup lemon juice
3 cloves garlic, crushed
2 teaspoons olive oil
2 teaspoons pepper, freshly ground
2 teaspoons tarragon
1 teaspoon thyme
¾ teaspoon salt

Place the chicken breasts in a large mixing bowl. Combine the remaining ingredients and pour over the chicken. Turn the breasts so they are coated with the seasoning mixture. Refrigerate the chicken in its marinade at least 1 hour, turning it occasionally. The marinade may be prepared ahead of time.

Preheat the oven broiler. Place the chicken breasts skin side down in an ovenproof baking dish. Place the dish 3 to 4 inches below the broiler. Broil 15 to 18 minutes on each side, basting occasionally with marinade.

SERVES 4.
150 CALORIES PER SERVING.

• Glazed Cauliflower

3 cups cauliflower, flowerets
½ cup low-fat cottage cheese
1 teaspoon lemon juice
1 teaspoon red wine vinegar
1 teaspoon onion, finely diced
2 tablespoons fresh parsley, finely chopped
1 teaspoon Parmesan cheese, grated
¼ teaspoon dry mustard
¼ teaspoon dill
1 teaspoon paprika (for garnish)

Boil 2 quarts of water. When it is at a full boil, add the flowerets. Reduce the heat and cover; simmer approximately 20 to 30 minutes, or until cauliflower is soft to the touch.

Combine the remaining ingredients and place in a blender; blend until smooth (this may be done ahead of time). Dip the cauliflower flowerets in the sauce and serve them glazed side up with a garnish of paprika. Serve hot or cold.

For variation, the cauliflower may be served whole; simply coat the entire cauliflower with the glaze.

Serves 4.
20 Calories per Serving.

• Green Salad with Italian Dressing

Green Salad
1 cucumber, thinly sliced
12 to 16 iceberg or romaine lettuce leaves
1 tomato, sliced into thin wedges

Place the cucumber on a bed of romaine or iceberg lettuce leaves, arranging the tomato wedges between the cucumber slices. Pour 2 tablespoons of the Italian Dressing (recipe follows) over the entire plate.

Serves 4.
23 Calories per Tablespoon of Dressing.

Italian Dressing

½ cup tomato juice

¼ cup safflower, corn, or olive oil

½ cup red wine vinegar

⅛ cup Parmesan cheese, grated

2 cloves garlic, crushed

½ teaspoon Dijon mustard

2 teaspoons oregano

2 teaspoons basil

¼ teaspoon black pepper, freshly ground

⅛ teaspoon cayenne pepper

Combine all of the dressing ingredients in a jar. Shake vigorously and chill for a few hours. The more time the herbs have to "age together," the more flavorful the dressing. The dressing may be stored in the refrigerator for up to 3 weeks.

DAY 3

● SALMON PASTA SALAD

1 cup canned salmon, chopped
⅓ cup celery, diced
⅓ cup fresh parsley, finely chopped
8–10 shallots (1 cup), peeled and minced
¼ cup pimiento, drained and chopped (optional)
1 cup cooked small pasta (or macaroni or spaghetti broken into small pieces)
2 tablespoons olive oil
juice of 1 lemon
⅓ teaspoon dry mustard
¼ cup fresh dill, chopped
salt and freshly ground pepper to taste

Place the fish in a large bowl. Add the celery, parsley, shallots, and pimiento. Toss well. Add the pasta and toss again.

Mix the oil, lemon juice, and mustard in a bowl until the mustard is a fully dissolved sauce. Mix in the dill, and pour the sauce over the fish and pasta. Salt and pepper to taste. Chill for about 20 minutes before serving.

Note: Alternate the salmon in this recipe with halibut, mahimahi, or tuna, canned or fresh.

SERVES 4.
225 CALORIES PER SERVING.

• NONFAT YOGURT

3 cups water
¾ cup nonfat, noninstant, powdered milk
¼ cup yogurt (use only *natural* yogurt without the additives)
½ cup fresh fruit, chopped (optional)

Preheat the oven to 115°F. Combine all the ingredients in a blender and blend. Pour the mixture into a quart jar and cover tightly. Place the jar in the oven and leave it for 4 hours. Chill for several hours, until it has a firm consistency.

Make the yogurt ahead of time and use it as you need it for sauces and dessert toppings. It may be served with banana slices and/or strawberries, raspberries, blueberries, or other fruit of choice to make a measured ½ cup serving per person.

MAKES 3 CUPS.
37 CALORIES PER ½ CUP OF PLAIN YOGURT; 71 CALORIES PER ½ CUP OF YOGURT WITH FRUIT.

• VICHYSSOISE

4 cups leeks, trimmed
1 tablespoon dry vermouth
1 cup potatoes, russet or red, peeled and sliced
2 cups cauliflower, chopped
4 cups chicken bouillon stock
¼ cup buttermilk
1 teaspoon dill
4 tablespoons scallions, finely chopped

Cut the leeks into ½-inch sections. In a small frying pan, sauté the leeks in the vermouth until limp (5 minutes). Combine the sautéed leeks, potatoes, cauliflower, and chicken stock in a pot and boil until the cauliflower and potatoes are completely tender (about 15 to 20 minutes). Add the buttermilk and dill to the mixture, stirring gently. Remove the soup from the heat and chill. To serve, top off each cup with 1 tablespoon chopped scallions. To thin soup, slowly stir in a little more buttermilk.

SERVES 4.
80 CALORIES PER SERVING.

• POACHED SALMON STEAK WITH DILL SAUCE

4 salmon fillets (about ⅓ pound each, raw weight)
¼–½ purple onion, thinly sliced to make 4 slices
½ cup dry vermouth
1–2 cups White Wine Court Bouillon (recipe follows) (or 1 cup clam juice
and 1 cup water)
⅛ teaspoon pepper, freshly ground
¼ teaspoon nutmeg
1 tablespoon fresh parsley, minced

Place salmon steaks in a baking dish or skillet and top each with 1 onion slice. Pour in wine and court bouillon. Bring slowly to a boil on top of the stove; then reduce the heat and cover. Simmer gently for 10 minutes. Top each salmon steak with a dollop of Dill Sauce (recipe follows, page 101). Top with a pinch of nutmeg, parsley, and pepper and serve.

SERVES 4.
352 CALORIES PER SERVING.

• WHITE WINE COURT BOUILLON

4 cups water
1 cup dry white wine
1 medium-sized onion, thinly sliced
2 medium-sized carrots, sliced
1 clove garlic, cut in half
1 large dried bay leaf, crumbled
½ teaspoon thyme
1 tablespoon pepper, freshly ground

Bring all the ingredients to a boil in a large saucepan. Simmer, uncovered, for 30 minutes. Cool and strain through a double thickness of dampened cheesecloth. Store in the refrigerator or freezer and use for poaching all varieties of fish.

MAKES 4 CUPS.

• DILL SAUCE

3 cups low-fat cottage cheese
1 cup buttermilk
2 tablespoons freshly squeezed lemon juice
1 cup fresh dill, chopped (or ½ cup dried dill)

Combine all the ingredients in a blender. Blend until mixture becomes smooth and creamy like sour cream. If the mixture is not creamy enough, slowly add buttermilk until you achieve desired effect.

Note: This low-fat recipe can also be used without the dill as a substitute for sour cream, or it can be used as a dessert topping by adding 1 tablespoon *concentrated* frozen orange juice or ¼ cup apple juice.

MAKES 1 QUART.
15 CALORIES PER TABLESPOON.

• ITALIAN RICE

1 cup long-grain rice
2 tablespoons olive oil
1 clove garlic, crushed
1 (10-ounce) package frozen chopped spinach, cooked and drained of excess liquid (or 2 cups fresh chopped spinach)
⅛ cup fresh parsley, finely chopped
¼ cup Parmesan cheese, grated
1 teaspoon salt
½ teaspoon pepper, freshly ground
1 teaspoon oregano
1 teaspoon thyme
1½ cups water

In a hot skillet, fry the rice in the olive oil and garlic until the rice becomes translucent. Reduce the heat to low and add the spinach, parsley, Parmesan cheese, and salt and pepper. Stir in the oregano and thyme and toss vigorously; add the water. Over a low flame, cook rice for 17 minutes, covered.

SERVES 4.
170 CALORIES PER SERVING.

DAY 4

●

• FOUR-BEAN SALAD

2 cups canned garbanzo beans, rinsed and drained
2 cups canned kidney beans, rinsed and drained
1 (10-ounce) can cut green beans
1 (10-ounce) can cut wax beans
1 stalk celery, finely chopped
1 small onion, finely chopped
1 tablespoon wine vinegar
1 teaspoon oregano
1 teaspoon basil
1 clove garlic, crushed or finely minced
1 tablespoon olive oil

In a large bowl combine all the beans; then add the celery, onion, vinegar, and herbs. Toss vigorously. Add oil and toss again. Chill for at least 1 hour, longer for fuller flavor.

SERVES 4.
284 CALORIES PER SERVING.

• TANDOORI CHICKEN

4 (4-ounce) boneless chicken breasts, skin and fat removed
1 cup plain nonfat yogurt
1 clove garlic, crushed or finely minced
1 teaspoon black pepper, freshly ground
¼ teaspoon cayenne pepper
2 tablespoons cider vinegar
1 teaspoon papaya, minced (optional)
1 teaspoon ground ginger
½ teaspoon ground coriander
½ teaspoon ground cumin seed
2 tablespoons lime juice
thin lemon slices

With a sharp knife, cut several slits on the chicken breasts. Mix all the other ingredients except the lemon slices. Marinate the chicken in this mixture for about 6 hours, or overnight, in the refrigerator.

Place the chicken breasts under the broiler and broil for 6 minutes, or until the chicken is lightly browned. Turn and broil for 6 more minutes or until the chicken is tender. Serve hot, garnished with thin lemon slices.

SERVES 4.
160 CALORIES PER SERVING.

• RICE PILAF

1 tablespoon soy sauce
2 tablespoons wild rice (may substitute thin spaghetti or vermicelli, cut into small pieces)
¼ cup brown rice
1 cup onion, finely chopped
1 cup bell pepper, finely chopped
1 cup water (or 1 cup chicken bouillon stock)
1 cup celery, finely diced
1 cup mushrooms, thinly sliced
1 teaspoon olive oil

Heat the soy sauce in a pan. To the hot soy sauce add the wild rice, brown rice, onion, and bell pepper. Raise the heat and stir-fry until the rice is coated with soy sauce. Add the water and return the rice to a simmer. Cover and simmer for 1 hour.

In a separate skillet, stir-fry the celery and mushrooms in the olive oil until just crunchy (al dente). Add to the cooked rice mixture, tossing gently. Let the pilaf sit for 15 minutes; then serve.

Note: This recipe calls for wild rice, but because it is not widely available, you may use thin spaghetti or vermicelli, cut into small pieces, placed in a medium-hot frying pan, and cooked until golden brown. Be careful not to burn.

SERVES 4.
60 CALORIES PER SERVING.

• BROCCOLI AND BEAN SPROUTS SAUTÉ

1½ tablespoons corn oil
1 pound broccoli, cut into small flowerets
½ tablespoon fresh ginger, grated (or 1 tablespoon dried ginger)
2 cloves garlic, finely chopped
10 ounces fresh bean sprouts
2 tablespoons soy sauce
1 teaspoon Chinese-style sesame oil

Heat the oil slightly in a large skillet, then add the broccoli flowerets, ginger, and garlic. Over a low flame, sauté for 2 minutes. Raise the heat to high, tossing the broccoli mixture vigorously, about 2 to 3 minutes. Add the bean sprouts and soy sauce. Toss vigorously until the bean sprouts soften, about 2 minutes. Remove from the flame, sprinkle on the sesame oil, and toss and serve.

SERVES 4.
50 CALORIES PER SERVING.

DAY 5

───────────────────────●───────────────────────

• GAZPACHO

1 (8-ounce) can tomato juice, unsalted
1 green chili, canned
½ cucumber, cubed
¼ bell pepper, diced
1 scallion
juice of ½ lemon
1 clove garlic, minced
1 teaspoon basil
¼ teaspoon oregano
pinch of coriander
1 teaspoon white vinegar
¼ cup fresh parsley, finely chopped
1 large tomato, finely diced

Combine all the ingredients except the parsley and diced tomato in a blender and liquefy. Just before serving, add the fresh parsley and finely diced tomato. Serve in chilled bowls and garnish with sprigs of parsley.

SERVES 4.
95 CALORIES PER SERVING.

• RICE SALAD NIÇOISE

2 cups water
1 cup long-grain rice
¾ cup Niçoise Salad Dressing (recipe follows, page 108)
2 (6½-ounce) cans chunk tuna, packed in water
1 cup celery, thinly sliced
1 cup cooked carrots, thinly sliced
⅓ cup toasted slivered almonds
½ cup sliced stuffed olives
⅓ cup capers
1 apple, red delicious, cut into finely sliced wedges

Bring the water to a boil. Stir in the rice. Reduce the heat and simmer, tightly covered, 17 minutes. Remove the rice from the heat and allow to stand, covered, 5 minutes; then drain and transfer to a large bowl. Add the dressing and gently blend. Refrigerate until chilled.

To serve, drain the tuna and combine the remaining ingredients. Toss thoroughly. Add the tuna mixture to the rice and toss until thoroughly blended.

SERVES 4.
432 CALORIES PER SERVING (DRESSING INCLUDED).

• NIÇOISE SALAD DRESSING

½ cup pure olive oil
⅓ cup wine vinegar
2 tablespoons fresh parsley, chopped
½ teaspoon basil
½ teaspoon dry mustard
1 clove garlic, crushed
¼ teaspoon paprika
⅛ teaspoon pepper, freshly ground
salt to taste

Measure all the ingredients into a blender. Cover tightly and blend. Refrigerate until chilled. Shake vigorously to serve. This dressing may be used on any kind of salad; it lasts about 3 weeks refrigerated.

MAKES 1 CUP.
75 CALORIES PER TABLESPOON.

• VEAL IN MUSHROOM AND TOMATO SAUCE

½ pound ripe plum tomatoes
1 tablespoon corn or safflower oil
2 shallots, finely chopped
1 clove garlic, minced
2 tablespoons dried seasonings (oregano, basil, rosemary, and garlic salt mixed together)
1 cup mushrooms, sliced
2 pounds veal, cubed
½ pound fresh okra
freshly ground black pepper to taste
2 tablespoons Parmesan cheese, freshly grated

Use firm, ripe, red tomatoes. Drop the tomatoes, one or two at a time, in boiling water to cover, and boil for exactly 10 seconds. Remove. Cut out the stems. Peel off the skin starting from the stem holes. Cut tomatoes in half crosswise, not through the stems. Squeeze each half gently to extract the seeds and juice from the center of the tomato. Now chop to make about 1 cup.

Pour the oil into a large frying pan over medium-high heat. Place the shallots and garlic in the pan and sauté until tender, or translucent in color. Add the seasonings, mushrooms, veal pieces, and okra, and sauté over high heat until the veal pieces are lightly browned. Add the chopped tomatoes; cover and simmer for 3 minutes. Sprinkle with Parmesan cheese and serve.

SERVES 4.
248 CALORIES PER SERVING.

• STUFFED POTATOES

2 large russet potatoes, scrubbed well
¾ cup buttermilk
1 clove garlic
1 teaspoon onion, finely chopped
¼ teaspoon pepper, freshly ground
¼ cup chives
paprika (for garnish)

Bake the potatoes for one hour at 350°F. Remove from the oven and increase the heat to broil. Cut the potatoes in half to make 4 equal shells, and scoop out the pulp into a blender. Add the buttermilk and dry ingredients, and whip until fluffy and light. Stuff the mixture into the potato skins; sprinkle with paprika. Place the stuffed potatoes under the broiler until the topping becomes golden brown.

SERVES 4.
50 CALORIES PER SERVING.

• ITALIAN VEGETABLE STIR-FRY

½ large green pepper, cut diagonally into ¼-inch slices
1 cup cauliflower, flowerets cubed
2 small zucchini, sliced into rounds
3 green onions, finely chopped
2 stalks celery, sliced on the diagonal
2 tomatoes, cut into wedges
1 teaspoon oregano
1 teaspoon basil
1 clove garlic, crushed
3 tablespoons chicken stock
¼ teaspoon pepper, freshly ground

Add the vegetables, herbs, and garlic to a moderately hot large frying pan. Immediately add the stock and cook, while stirring, for 5 minutes, or until vegetables are tender but still crispy. Add pepper and serve.

SERVES 4.
40 CALORIES PER SERVING.

DAY 6

●

• TOSSED SHREDDED CHICKEN SALAD

1 pound chicken breasts
½ cup canned chicken broth
1 medium-sized head iceberg lettuce, shredded (may substitute any other lettuce, shredded)
4 green onions, thinly sliced
1 small bunch cilantro, coarsely chopped
1 (4-ounce) can water chestnuts, very thinly sliced
1 stalk celery, very thinly sliced
½ cup canned petite peas (optional)
3 radishes, very thinly sliced
1 tablespoon Sesame Oil Dressing (recipe follows, page 112)
¼ cup toasted sesame seeds (place on medium heat in dry skillet and heat until browned but not burned)
1 avocado, sliced (or 4 fresh pineapple slices or spears)

Poach the chicken breasts in the broth for 15 minutes, or until they are cooked through. Let cool; then remove and discard the skin and bones, and dice the meat finely. Reserve the broth. Place the meat in a bowl with the lettuce, onion, cilantro, water chestnuts, celery, peas, and radishes. Pour the Sesame Oil Dressing over the salad and mix well. Spoon the salad onto plates and sprinkle with toasted sesame seeds. Garnish with avocado slices or fresh pineapple.

SERVES 4.
310 CALORIES PER SERVING (DRESSING INCLUDED).

• SESAME OIL DRESSING

1 teaspoon salt
½ teaspoon Tabasco sauce
½ teaspoon dry mustard
½ teaspoon grated lemon peel
1½ teaspoons white wine vinegar
1 teaspoon honey
1 teaspoon soy sauce
2 tablespoons sesame oil
1 tablespoon lemon juice
1 tablespoon corn or safflower oil

Place all the ingredients in a jar and shake vigorously.

MAKES ⅓ CUP.
75 CALORIES PER TABLESPOON.

• STEAMED FISH, CHINESE-STYLE

2 tablespoons fresh ginger, grated (may substitute dried ginger)
2 tablespoons peanut, sesame, or corn oil
1 tablespoon dry sherry (or Madeira) (optional)
1 tablespoon soy sauce
½ small white onion, cut into pieces
6 dried black mushrooms (soaked in water at least 15 minutes)
1¼ pounds whitefish, whole, fillets, or steaks
white pepper
chopped chives or scallion tops

Place the ginger, oil, sherry, soy sauce, onion, and mushrooms in a blender. Blend 2 or 3 seconds. Rub the fish on all sides with the white pepper, and sprinkle the blended sauce on all sides of the fish; then sprinkle with chopped chives or scallion tops.

Pour 2 inches of boiling water into a roaster pan. When the water is steaming in a lively fashion, put the fish on an ovenproof platter and place it on a rack set above the boiling water. Cook, covered, 10 to 15 minutes for a fish 2 inches thick; cook 4 to 6 minutes for fish fillets or small fish steaks.

SERVES 4.
440 CALORIES PER SERVING.

• FRIED RICE

3 cups cold cooked rice, steamed
1 egg
1 teaspoon cold water
¼ cup corn, safflower, or peanut oil
1½ cups celery, thinly sliced
1 cup cooked chicken, diced
1 cup fresh bean sprouts
½ cup scallions, thinly sliced
¼ cup soy sauce
¾ teaspoon ginger
1 clove garlic, finely minced or crushed

Steam the rice by taking 1½ cups rice and rinsing it in a colander 3 times. Place the drained rice in a pot and add 1½ cups water. Cover and simmer for 20 to 25 minutes on low-medium heat until the rice has steamed fully. Do not take the cover off during the cooking process.

Meanwhile, beat the egg lightly with the cold water. Heat 2 tablespoons oil in a medium-sized skillet and add the egg. Cook over medium heat, without stirring, to make a pancake. Turn once, cooking until the egg sets. Remove to a plate and cut into thin strips.

Heat the remaining oil in a large skillet over medium heat. Add the rice and celery; sauté until coated with oil. Add the remaining ingredients and cook, stirring gently, until thoroughly heated. Garnish the fried rice with egg strips before serving.

SERVES 4.
200 CALORIES PER CUP.

DAY 7

———————————————————●———————————————————

• CUCUMBERS IN YOGURT

2 medium cucumbers, pared, seeded, and thinly sliced
1 cup plain or low-fat yogurt
2 cloves garlic, finely minced or crushed
4 green onions or scallions, chopped
2 tablespoons fresh mint (or dried mint)
¼ teaspoon cumin
¼ teaspoon pepper, freshly ground
½ teaspoon lemon juice
4 tomato wedges (for garnish)
8 lettuce leaves, any type (for garnish) (optional)

Place the cucumbers in a colander and let stand an hour to allow excess water to drain; then rinse in cold water and drain well. Place the yogurt in a small bowl. Add the garlic and mix thoroughly. Now fold in the remaining ingredients. Garnish with the tomato wedges and serve immediately on a bed of lettuce leaves.

SERVES 4.
185 CALORIES PER SERVING.

• FRESH ORANGE FRUIT CUPS

2 oranges
½ banana, sliced
1 apple, diced
4 teaspoons raisins
4 tablespoons plain nonfat yogurt
1 tablespoon cinnamon

Cut the oranges in half. With a grapefruit knife or spoon, remove the fruit from the rind, leaving the rind intact; reserve for later use. Cut the orange segments into a bowl. Add the banana, apple, raisins, yogurt, and cinnamon, and mix well. Take the reserved "orange cup" rinds and fill with the fruit mixture. Chill and serve.

SERVES 4.
73 CALORIES PER SERVING.

• PASTA PRIMAVERA

1 pound pasta (thin spaghetti or green spinach noodles)
3 tablespoons corn, safflower, or peanut oil
1 pound unpeeled zucchini, cut julienne style and diced
1 pound ripe unpeeled plum tomatoes, diced (or 3 pounds canned imported
Italian plum tomatoes, drained and finely chopped)
6 shallots, peeled and finely diced
4 large mushrooms, thinly sliced
½ cup broccoli, chopped flowerets
¼ cup fresh parsley, finely chopped
2 small cloves garlic, finely minced or crushed
2 tablespoons fresh basil leaves, minced (or 1 tablespoon dried basil)
1 tablespoon oregano
1 tablespoon pepper, freshly ground
⅛ cup Parmesan cheese, freshly grated

Fill a large pot with cold water. Bring to a boil over high heat. Add salt, if desired. Then add the pasta and cook, stirring occasionally, just until the pasta is al dente. Drain the pasta in a colander and quickly rinse with cold water to stop the cooking process.

Pour the oil into a large skillet. Add the zucchini, tomatoes, shallots, mushrooms, broccoli, parsley, garlic, basil, oregano, and pepper. Turn on the heat to medium-high and sauté, stirring often with a wooden spoon to prevent burning. Cook 8 to 10 minutes. Pour the sauce over the pasta and serve. Add the Parmesan cheese and toss.

SERVES 4.
420 CALORIES PER SERVING.

• ASPARAGUS WITH LEMON-PARSLEY SAUCE

20–24 fresh asparagus spears
¼ cup lemon juice
2 tablespoons fresh parsley, chopped

Trim the bottoms of the asparagus spears and wash well. Tie them loosely together in a bunch. Stand the asparagus upright in 2 inches of water in a deep pot and cover. In this way the tender tops steam as the bottoms boil. Cook about 10 minutes, or until tender. Remove the spears from the water and arrange on a platter. Mix the lemon juice and parsley and pour over the asparagus. Serve immediately. The sauce may be prepared ahead of time.

SERVES 4.
25 CALORIES PER SERVING.

• GARLIC BREAD

4 (4- by 8-inch) slices Italian or French-style bread
2 cloves garlic
1 teaspoon basil
2 teaspoons Parmesan cheese, grated

Toast the bread slices. Take the *raw* garlic cloves and rub them across the entire surface of each bread slice. Top each with a pinch of basil and Parmesan cheese and serve.

For a less austere version of this Italian low-fat specialty, *lightly* brush the garlic-flavored surface with a thin film of olive oil.

SERVES 4.
87 CALORIES FOR 1 SLICE.

DAY 8

━━━━━━━━━━━━━━━━━━━━━━━━●━━━━━━━━━━━━━━━━━━━━━

• CHICKEN RELLENO

½ cup onion, finely chopped
1 clove garlic, finely minced or crushed
1 cup tomato sauce (low-salt, if available)
1 teaspoon basil
1 teaspoon oregano
1 teaspoon chili powder
2 whole chicken breasts
½ cup water
1 small *can* whole green chilis (seeded)
1 cup mozzarella cheese, grated

Preheat the oven to 350°F. Combine the onion, garlic, tomato sauce, and spices in a saucepan. Cover and simmer approximately 1 hour. Meanwhile, strip the chicken of its skin and fat; then poach in the water for 15 minutes. As the chicken cooks, drain some of the broth and add to the sauce to prevent the sauce from thickening or drying out. After allowing it to cool, debone and slice the chicken lengthwise. Layer the chicken on the bottom of a nonstick pan; then add the chilis and top with the mozzarella cheese. Pour the sauce evenly to cover all the cheese. Bake 30 minutes.

Note: You can make this dish ahead of time and simply reheat it in the oven or microwave.

SERVES 4.
210 CALORIES PER SERVING.

• SKEWERED SWORDFISH

3 tablespoons dry vermouth (or dry white wine)
1½ tablespoons lemon juice
1 tablespoon olive oil
½ teaspoon salt
½ teaspoon oregano
1 clove garlic, minced
1 green onion, chopped
1 pound swordfish or halibut steaks, cut about ¾-inch thick
12 cherry tomatoes
12 fresh bay leaves (if available)
1 lemon, cut into wedges (for garnish)

In a large bowl combine the vermouth, lemon juice, oil, salt, oregano, garlic, and onion. Cut the fish into 1¼-inch squares, place in the marinade, cover, and refrigerate 1 hour, turning every 15 minutes.

Preheat the oven to 350°F. Alternate on skewers the fish, tomatoes, and bay leaves; use only freshly picked bay leaves or omit, as dry ones will burn. Place the skewered fish on a broiler pan in the oven and broil about 10 minutes, turning every 2 to 3 minutes and basting with marinade. Serve with lemon wedges.

SERVES 4.
157 CALORIES PER SERVING.

• RICE WITH GREEN PEPPERS AND MUSHROOMS

2 tablespoons corn oil margarine
1 cup mushrooms, chopped
1 cup green pepper, chopped
1 clove garlic, crushed
1 cup long-grain rice
1½ cups chicken bouillon
¼ teaspoon pepper, freshly ground
3 tablespoons fresh parsley, chopped

Preheat the oven to 375°F. Melt the margarine in an ovenproof glass pan or bowl over a low flame. Add the mushrooms, green pepper, and garlic. Sauté until the mushrooms are tender. Add the rice. Mix gently. Stir in the chicken bouillon and pepper, and bring to a boil. Remove from the heat, cover tightly, and place in the oven and bake 20 minutes, or until the liquid is absorbed. Add parsley. Stir gently to blend before serving.

SERVES 6.
173 CALORIES PER SERVING.

• STRAWBERRY-RASPBERRY SOUP

3 cups fresh strawberries (or frozen, drained)
3 cups fresh raspberries (or frozen, drained)
⅓ cup apple juice
2 tablespoons cornstarch
¾ cup water
1 tablespoon lemon juice
¼ cup sour cream
¼ cup plain low-fat yogurt
1 teaspoon powdered sugar
½ teaspoon vanilla

Cut the strawberries in half. Place the strawberries, raspberries, and apple juice in a large saucepan and let stand 15 minutes. Heat over low heat to boiling. Mix together the cornstarch and water, and stir in. Stirring constantly, boil the mixture until the fruits soften and the soup is clear and thickened. Remove from the heat and stir in the lemon juice. Chill. (The soup may be prepared 1 day in advance to this point.)

Spoon the soup into small bowls. Just before serving, blend together the sour cream, yogurt, powdered sugar, and vanilla. Garnish each serving with 1 tablespoon of this topping.

SERVES 8.
100 CALORIES PER SERVING.

DAY 9

• **ALASKA-STYLE COBB SALAD**

1 (7¾-ounce) can Alaska salmon (alternate with tuna, fresh or canned)
1½ cups romaine lettuce, chopped
1½ cups iceberg lettuce, chopped
1 small tomato, cubed
¼ medium avocado, diced
2 green onions, finely chopped
2 tablespoons blue cheese, crumbled
1 tablespoon Dijon Dressing (recipe follows)

Drain the salmon and reserve 2 tablespoons of the liquid for the Dijon Dressing. Flake the salmon. Combine the lettuce, and create a bed of this mixture on a platter. Arrange the salmon, tomato, avocado, onion, and cheese in rows on top of the lettuce. Serve with Dijon Dressing.

SERVES 2.
400 CALORIES PER SERVING (DRESSING INCLUDED).

• **DIJON DRESSING**

1 tablespoon corn oil
2 tablespoons white wine vinegar
2 tablespoons salmon liquid (reserved from preceding recipe)
1 teaspoon fresh parsley, chopped
1 teaspoon Dijon mustard
¾ teaspoon grated lemon rind
¼ teaspoon thyme

Combine all the ingredients in a small jar; shake vigorously until well mixed. May be stored in the refrigerator for up to 1 week.

MAKES ⅓ CUP.
30 CALORIES PER TABLESPOON.

• BAKED APPLE CRUNCH

½ tablespoon sesame seeds, toasted
1 cup bran
2 tablespoons wheat germ
1½ tablespoons cinnamon
1 tablespoon corn oil (or nonstick spray)
5 apples, cored and thinly sliced
juice of 1 lemon

Preheat the oven to 350°F. Crush the sesame seeds. Combine the bran, wheat germ, and cinnamon, and mix well in a bowl. Coat an 8-inch glass baking dish with corn oil or nonstick spray. Sprinkle half the bran mixture on the bottom of the dish to form a thin layer. Layer half the sliced apples over the bran layer and sprinkle with lemon juice. Form another layer with the remaining bran mixture. Top with the remaining sliced apples and sprinkle with sesame seeds and lemon juice. Cover tightly with foil. Bake for 1½ hours. Chill, cut into squares, and serve. This is very good with a little yogurt topping.

SERVES 6.
70 CALORIES PER SERVING.

• NEW ORLEANS SEAFOOD STEW

⅛ cup olive oil
1 medium-sized yellow onion, finely diced
½ small green pepper, finely diced
1 cup celery, finely diced
1 (16-ounce) can stewed tomatoes, diced
2 (8-ounce) cans tomato sauce
½ cup dry white wine
1 cup water
6 sprigs fresh parsley, finely chopped
2 cloves garlic, crushed
½ teaspoon ground cumin
¼ teaspoon oregano
½ teaspoon cayenne
½ teaspoon salt
½ teaspoon pepper, freshly ground
2 cups potatoes, cubed
1 (6-ounce) can whole clams (juice reserved)
1½ pounds raw red snapper, cubed
⅓ pound small cooked shrimp

In the oil sauté the onion, green pepper, and celery over a low flame until they're lightly browned. Add the stewed tomatoes, tomato sauce, wine, water, parsley, garlic, cumin, oregano, cayenne, salt, and pepper. Cover the sauce and simmer for 5 minutes. Add the potatoes, clams, and clam juice. After simmering for 15 minutes, add the red snapper and shrimp. Simmer until the potatoes are soft, about 2 to 3 minutes. Do not overcook; snapper should remain firm.

SERVES 6.
246 CALORIES PER SERVING.

• RICE AND MUSHROOMS

2 quarts water
1 cup brown rice
3 tablespoons carrots, finely minced
3 tablespoons onion, finely minced
3 tablespoons celery, finely minced
½ pound mushrooms, sliced
¼ cup dry white wine
1½ cups canned beef stock or bouillon
1 dried bay leaf
2 teaspoons thyme
⅛ teaspoon pepper, freshly ground

Preheat the oven to 350°F. Bring the water to a boil and drop the rice into the boiling water. Boil uncovered for 5 minutes. Drain the rice. Meanwhile, in an ovenproof pan or dish, sauté the carrots, onion, celery, and mushrooms in the white wine. Add the sautéed vegetables, bouillon, and remaining seasonings to the rice. Bring to a rolling boil and boil for 1 minute. Cover the dish and put it in the preheated oven for 35 minutes, or until the rice is tender. Add a few drops more liquid if all the liquid has been absorbed before the rice is tender. Remove the bay leaf and serve.

SERVES 4.
86 CALORIES PER SERVING.

• "PUMPKIN" PIE

1 cup butternut squash, peeled, seeded, and roughly chopped (or canned pumpkin)
2 tablespoons honey
2 teaspoons molasses
1 teaspoon cinnamon
1 egg yolk
⅛ teaspoon ginger
⅛ teaspoon nutmeg
2 egg whites

Preheat the oven to 350°F. Cook the squash in boiling water until very soft (if you're using canned pumpkin, avoid this step); then puree in a blender. Add the honey, molasses, cinnamon, egg yolk, ginger, and nutmeg to the mixture in the blender and mix well. Whip the egg whites until they form peaks. Fold the squash mixture into the whipped egg whites. Pour into a pie pan. Bake for 1 hour, and cool.

SERVES 8.
55 CALORIES PER SERVING.

DAY 10

• CHICKEN IN PITA BREAD

¼ pound cooked chicken, shredded (may substitute water-packed tuna)
2 tablespoons fresh chives, finely chopped
½ cup iceberg lettuce, shredded
½ small tomato, diced
¼ teaspoon garlic powder
1 tablespoon vinegar, any type
1 whole-wheat pita
1 tablespoon Fast Salsa (see page 147)

Combine the chicken, chives, lettuce, tomato, and garlic powder and mix with the vinegar. Cut off the top ⅛ inch of the pita and set aside. Stuff the mixture into the pita bread and serve.

SERVES 1.
435 CALORIES PER SERVING.

• CREAMY ORANGE-PEANUT DIP

1 cup low-fat cottage cheese
2 tablespoons smooth peanut butter
2 tablespoons frozen orange juice concentrate

Blend all the ingredients together until smooth. Serve with crudités. This dip makes carrots, celery, and apple slices taste fattening.

MAKES 1 CUP.
16 CALORIES PER TABLESPOON.

• SEAFOOD KABOBS

3 tablespoons lemon juice
1 tablespoon dry vermouth
1 tablespoon olive oil
2 cloves garlic, crushed
1 tablespoon fresh parsley, chopped
1 green onion, finely chopped
1 teaspoon oregano
1 teaspoon salt
¼ teaspoon pepper, freshly ground
1½ pounds large fresh shrimp (or a 1½-pound mixture of shrimp and scallops)
8 cherry tomatoes
1 green pepper, cut into 1-inch cubes
8 metal skewers
15 sprigs fresh cilantro, chopped

Mix together the lemon juice, vermouth, olive oil, garlic, parsley, onion, oregano, salt, and pepper. Clean the shrimp, leaving the tail shells intact, and split the shrimp meat halfway to the tail, washing out the vein. Let marinate in the dressing for 30 minutes, turning occasionally. Thread each of the skewers alternately with the cherry tomatoes, green pepper, and 2 or 3 shrimp. Barbecue over medium-hot coals or on an indoor grill, turning for 4 to 5 minutes, or until shrimp turn pink and curl up. Sprinkle with cilantro and serve.

SERVES 4.
81 CALORIES PER SERVING.

• EGGPLANT OVER PASTA

½ teaspoon garlic powder
1 medium eggplant (1 pound), sliced into ½-inch sections
½ teaspoon dried oregano
1 teaspoon basil
½ teaspoon pepper
8 ounces hoop cheese
2 medium tomatoes, peeled and thinly sliced
4 ounces onion, thinly sliced
1 medium green pepper, cut into thin strips
4 tablespoons Parmesan cheese, grated
8 ounces whole-wheat spaghetti

Preheat the oven to 350°F. Sprinkle the garlic powder over the eggplant. Mix the oregano, basil, and pepper with the hoop cheese. In a deep casserole dish alternate layers of eggplant, tomato, onion, green pepper, and hoop cheese mixed with spices. Sprinkle Parmesan cheese over the hoop cheese on each layer. Repeat layers, ending with the cheese. Cover and bake for 20 minutes; uncover and continue to bake another 30 minutes until eggplant is done. Serve the baked eggplant casserole over cooked pasta.

SERVES 4.
360 CALORIES PER SERVING.

• STRAWBERRY ICE

1 quart ripe strawberries
¼ cup water
1 cup sugar
2 tablespoons lemon juice

In a medium saucepan combine the strawberries and water and cook over medium-high heat for 5 minutes, or until berries are soft. Gently blend this mixture until smooth. Whip in the sugar and lemon juice. Chill.

When cold, pour the mixture into a wide bowl and place in the freezer. Once a frozen texture begins to form, stir well and return to the freezer. Repeat this procedure two to three times, so that the mixture assumes the texture of sherbet. Cover and freeze for several hours. For best flavor, remove the Strawberry Ice from the freezer and let sit in the refrigerator for about 15 minutes before serving.

SERVES 6.
161 CALORIES PER ½ CUP.

DAY 11

• TABOULI SALAD

1 cup bulgur wheat
1 cup boiling water
1 cup fresh parsley, finely chopped
½ cup green onion, finely chopped
1 pound tomatoes, coarsely chopped
¼ cup dried mint
⅓ cup lemon juice
¼ teaspoon pepper, freshly ground
4 romaine lettuce leaves (for garnish)

Cover the bulgur wheat with the boiling water, set aside, and let soak for 2 hours. Drain well. Add the remaining ingredients and toss together. Cover and let stand overnight in the refrigerator. Serve on a bed of romaine lettuce.

SERVES 4.
100 CALORIES PER SERVING.

• EGGPLANT PARMIGIANA

1 medium-sized eggplant
2 tablespoons olive oil
3 shallots, peeled and chopped
½ pound ripe plum tomatoes, cored and diced
2 tablespoons parsley
2 tablespoons basil
¼ cup Parmesan cheese, freshly grated
2 ounces part-skim mozzarella
1 teaspoon salt

Preheat the broiler. Wash and peel the eggplant, and cut it length-wise into ¼-inch slices. Soak the slices in a bowl of cold salty water for 10 minutes; then rinse in fresh cold water. Pat the slices dry.

Brush a few drops of the olive oil on a baking sheet, and arrange the eggplant slices on the sheet in a single layer. Brush the tops with a light coating of olive oil. Broil for 5 minutes, set aside.

Preheat the oven to 350°F. Heat the remaining 1 tablespoon olive oil in a small frying pan and add the shallots. Sauté for 1 minute; then add the tomatoes and herbs. Cook for 10 minutes over a low flame, stirring occasionally. Pour the sauce into a large baking dish. Arrange the eggplant slices on top of the sauce in a single layer. Sprinkle with the Parmesan cheese. Shred the mozzarella and sprinkle it over the eggplant. Bake for another 15 minutes.

SERVES 4.
135 CALORIES PER SERVING.

• BROILED TOMATO PARMESAN

3 medium-sized tomatoes
2 tablespoons Parmesan cheese, finely grated
2 tablespoons bread crumbs
1 tablespoon parsley, finely chopped

Preheat the broiler. Cut the tomatoes in half and place on a cookie sheet. Combine cheese and bread crumbs; then sprinkle over tomato halves and place under the broiler for 10 minutes until brown. Serve with a sprinkle of chopped parsley.

SERVES 4 TO 6.
25 CALORIES PER SERVING.

DAY 12

• CLAM CHOWDER

1½ cups water
1 cup russet potatoes, peeled and cubed
2 cups cauliflower, flowerets
1 cup white onion, finely chopped
2 tablespoons arrowroot (or 1 tablespoon cornstarch)
1 cup buttermilk
1 teaspoon dill
¼ teaspoon marjoram
1 (6-ounce) can small clams
¼ cup fresh or dried chives

Add the water and vegetables to a soup pot. Place on high heat until boiling. Cook 15 minutes, stirring constantly. Remove from the heat and lightly mash the vegetables with a fork, leaving some chunks. Dissolve the arrowroot in buttermilk; then add the dill and marjoram. Add to the soup and stir over low heat until the soup is thick. Add the clams with juice and stir just until hot. Do not let it boil. Serve as soon as the soup is hot; sprinkle each serving with chives.

SERVES 4.
73 CALORIES PER SERVING.

• BRAN MUFFINS

1 cup stone-ground whole-wheat flour
1 teaspoon baking soda
1¾ cups bran
½ teaspoon ground cinnamon
⅛ teaspoon ground cloves
⅛ teaspoon nutmeg
½ teaspoon vanilla
½ cup frozen apple juice concentrate, defrosted
1 egg white
¾ cup skim milk
¼ cup fresh blueberries (or frozen unsweetened blueberries, drained)

Preheat the oven to 400°F. Mix together all the ingredients except the blueberries, egg white, and skim milk. Next add the egg white and milk and stir until smooth. Gently fold in the blueberries. Pour mixture into muffin tins. Bake for 20 to 30 minutes.

MAKES 24 MUFFINS.
88 CALORIES PER MUFFIN.

• BROCCOLI SOUP

2 cups canned chicken broth (or chicken bouillon)
2 cups broccoli, 1-inch flowerets
½ teaspoon basil (or ½ teaspoon tarragon or ½–1 teaspoon curry powder)
1 tablespoon lemon juice
¼ cup milk powder (optional, see below)
1 teaspoon fresh chives
1 teaspoon parsley

Put the chicken broth in a large pot and bring to a boil. Put the broccoli immediately into boiling broth and stir. When the soup returns to a full boil, remove from heat. Season with basil, tarragon, or curry powder to taste. Let cool. Place the soup in a blender; add lemon juice and puree. (This can be made into a cream-style soup by adding milk powder right before blending.) Garnish each serving with chives and/or parsley.

SERVES 4.
14 CALORIES PER SERVING. (20 calories per serving if milk powder is added.)

• BROILED HERBED CHICKEN

½ pound boneless chicken, skin and fat removed
2 tablespoons frozen orange juice concentrate, defrosted
½ teaspoon tarragon vinegar
1 teaspoon oregano
¼ teaspoon parsley
1 teaspoon basil
¼ teaspoon dry mustard

Preheat the broiler. Arrange the chicken in a broiler pan. In a bowl combine all the ingredients and mix well. Brush half the mixture over the chicken. Broil for 6 minutes, or until the chicken is lightly browned. Turn and baste with the remaining herb mixture. Broil for 6 minutes more, or until chicken is tender.

SERVES 2.
320 CALORIES PER SERVING.

• SAUTÉED ZUCCHINI AND CARROTS

½ pound carrots
½ pound zucchini
1 tablespoon olive, corn, or safflower oil
1 clove garlic, finely minced
2 tablespoons fresh parsley, finely chopped

Rinse the vegetables, cut off the ends (*do not* peel), and slice julienne style. Add the oil and garlic to a pan and heat over medium heat. Cook until the oil beads around the garlic. Add the carrots and sauté for 2 minutes; then add the zucchini and half the chopped parsley. Continue to sauté, stirring occasionally, for 3 more minutes. Remove from heat; add remaining parsley and toss lightly. Transfer the vegetables to a serving dish.

SERVES 4.
40 CALORIES PER SERVING.

• VEGETABLE SOUP

10 sprigs fresh parsley
1 bay leaf
1 teaspoon pepper, freshly ground
1 large (28-ounce) can tomatoes, quartered
1 medium-sized onion, diced
½ medium-sized lemon, sliced
2 cloves garlic, crushed
¼ teaspoon allspice
6 cups water
½ cup green peppers, shredded
½ cup carrots, shredded
½ cup cabbage, shredded

Put the parsley, bay leaf, pepper, tomatoes, onion, lemon, garlic, and allspice into a large pot. Add the water and bring to a boil. Reduce the heat, cover, and simmer for 30 minutes. Puree in a blender. Return the soup to the pot and bring to medium heat. Stir in the green peppers, carrots, and cabbage. Simmer until the carrots are tender. Serve hot.

SERVES 4.
46 CALORIES PER SERVING.

• SZECHUAN SALAD

¼ cup canned beef broth (or beef bouillon)
2 cups broccoli, flowerets
1 sweet red bell pepper, thinly sliced
1 cup mushrooms, thinly sliced
2 tablespoons Chinese-style sesame oil
4 tablespoons white vinegar
2 tablespoons soy sauce (low-salt if available)
1 clove garlic, crushed
¼ tablespoon fresh ginger, grated
½ teaspoon red pepper, crushed, dried
4 ounces rare lean roast beef, thinly sliced julienne style
½ (8-ounce) can water chestnuts, drained
½ (8-ounce) can bamboo shoots, drained

In a large nonstick skillet or wok heat ⅛ cup of beef broth or bouillon. Add the broccoli and stir-fry until the broccoli becomes tender but is still crisp (about 3 minutes). Transfer the broccoli to a bowl. Stir-fry the sweet red pepper strips in the same pan over moderate heat for 1 to 2 minutes. Add more beef broth as needed. Transfer to the broccoli bowl. Repeat with the mushrooms and add to the cooked broccoli–red pepper mix. In a small glass jar or container with a top, mix the sesame oil, vinegar, soy sauce, garlic, ginger, and red pepper (to taste). Shake; then pour over the broccoli-pepper-mushroom mixture. Toss gently. Add the roast beef strips, water chestnuts, and bamboo shoots to the vegetable mixture and toss gently. Cover and refrigerate for 3 hours before serving.

Note: This can be made the night before. The salad becomes somewhat more flavorful if kept refrigerated for 24 hours.

SERVES 4.
334 CALORIES PER SERVING.

• EGG FOO YOUNG

2 green onions, tops included, minced
½ cup bell pepper, finely chopped
¼ cup celery, finely chopped
¼ cup mushrooms, thinly sliced
2 cups bean sprouts, chopped
4 eggs
1 tablespoon soy sauce (low-salt if available)
⅓ teaspoon fresh ginger, grated (or ⅔ teaspoon ginger powder)
1 clove garlic, finely minced (or ⅓ teaspoon garlic powder)
nonstick spray

Mix the vegetables in a bowl. Combine the eggs, soy sauce, ginger, and garlic and beat lightly; mix with the vegetables. Make into 4-inch pancakes. Brown on each side on a hot griddle, using nonstick spray on the griddle.

SERVES 4.
67 CALORIES PER SERVING.

• FRUIT CUP

3 teaspoons frozen orange juice concentrate, defrosted
1 teaspoon lemon juice (to taste)
1 teaspoon frozen apple juice concentrate, defrosted (to taste)
1 medium-sized apple, cored and diced
1 medium-sized orange, diced
1 medium-sized banana, sliced
½ cup seedless grapes, halved
½ cup blueberries (fresh or frozen)
2 teaspoons walnuts, chopped (optional)
2 teaspoons grated coconut (optional)

Pour the orange juice concentrate, lemon juice, and apple juice concentrate into a bowl and mix in the fruits. Chill. Garnish each serving with chopped walnuts and/or coconut.

SERVES 4.
76 CALORIES PER SERVING.

DAY 14

———————————————————●———————————————————

● STRING BEAN TUNA SALAD

2 cups canned water-packed tuna
1 cup canned string beans, chopped
1 cup canned kidney beans
1 medium-sized onion, chopped
2 cloves garlic, finely minced or crushed
¼ cup wine vinegar (may substitute cider vinegar)
¼ cup water
1 tablespoon lemon juice

Drain the tuna of excess water. Drain the beans and rinse thoroughly with cold water. Combine the beans, tuna, onion, and garlic. Cover with the vinegar, water, and lemon juice. Toss gently; then chill in the refrigerator. The salad may be made the night before serving.

SERVES 4.
258 CALORIES PER SERVING.

• CHICKEN TOSTADA

8 corn tortillas
1 teaspoon chili powder
1 teaspoon oregano
½ teaspoon cumin
2 quarts water
2 cloves garlic
1 pound whole chicken
⅔ cup tomato sauce
2 tablespoons onion, finely chopped
2 drops Tabasco sauce
3 cups iceberg lettuce, shredded
⅔ cup fresh tomato, finely chopped
⅔ cup cheddar cheese, grated

Preheat the oven to 450°F. Bake the tortillas for 10 to 15 minutes, until they brown and become hard. Set aside. Combine the chili powder, oregano, and cumin. Place the water and garlic cloves in a pot and bring to a boil. Add the whole chicken and boil for 10 minutes. Shred when cool.

Mix the tomato sauce, onion, and Tabasco sauce in a large saucepan. Add the seasonings and shredded chicken; simmer for 5 minutes. Take each tortilla and layer with the chicken-sauce mixture, lettuce, and tomato. Top with grated cheese.

SERVES 4.
145 CALORIES PER SERVING.

• SPANISH BROWN RICE

1¾ cups water
1 cup brown rice
½ cup green pepper, finely chopped
½ cup onion, finely chopped
4 ounces tomato paste
½ teaspoon chili powder
¼ teaspoon cumin
1 teaspoon pepper, freshly ground (optional)

Bring the water to a rolling boil and add the rice, stirring well. Add the remaining ingredients and stir. When the rice returns to a boil, reduce the heat, cover, and simmer for 50 minutes. Let cool 20 minutes and serve.

SERVES 4.
56 CALORIES PER SERVING.

14.

The Fish-Centered Way to Good Health

By following the fourteen-day *Omega-3*–based rapid-weight-loss program on The Good Fat Diet, you've kept to a highly restricted plan that allows you to lose five to seven pounds. This very restriction explains why this rapid weight loss occurs in the first place. But now you have a new goal: to maintain your weight loss and integrate this healthy eating program into your life. Here it should be remembered that despite the "miracle doctors" who claim that calories don't count, be assured that by all the medical and dietary evidence they very much do. Remember, The Good Fat Diet by itself is no panacea to weight loss—you still have to keep track of the calories.

Fortunately, by going from a meat- to a fish-centered diet, the task of calorie control becomes infinitely easier. On The Good Fat Diet you've learned to prepare fish in many different ways—poaching, steaming, stir-frying, and grilling. Low-calorie cooking, in fact, is at the heart of The Good Fat Diet. And by continuing to eat the variety of meals high in the good *Omega-3* fish fats, you not only keep unwanted body weight from creeping back up, but more important, you have made a crucial decision for your health by reducing the bad fat buildup in the arteries. This has occurred as a result of shifting the protein source from items that are both high in protein and high in bad animal fats to foods that are both high in protein and high in the good *Omega-3* fish fat.

For perfect weight maintenance your intake of calories should be between 2200 and 2500 a day. The task of keeping to this average is easily accomplished by the techniques and ideas taught by The Good Fat Diet. If you were not one before, you are probably now a very creative fish cook.

Nutritionists generally recommend that the healthful American diet include two fish dishes a week. However, we recommend that, in order to keep the good *Omega-3* working in the system, it's preferable to eat at least three or as many as four fish dishes a week. With this heavy representation of fish dishes on the menu, my husband and I have found it important to keep on hand a great many accompaniments and flavorings. Different herbs, wines, and sauces do wonders, we've discovered, in keeping the fish-centered menu exciting and varied. What follows represents a selection of our own favorite fish dishes, along with a few of our favorite low-fat side dishes and dips.

Apart from main dishes, like the delicious Paella, you will find zesty low-calorie dips, such as the salsa and curry; and sauces that *taste* fattening that are low in calories, such as a tartar sauce for fish, or that are made with unusual flavorings like yogurt or cilantro. You will also find a few of our favorite side dishes to accompany the high-fish-fat eating plan—oven-fried potatoes, for instance, instead of french fries or au gratin.

Among these supplemental recipes you will notice that main dishes like grilled trout, or halibut with basil—or a rich-tasting Cioppino—are a little outnumbered in favor of salmon. That's because salmon is both delicious *and* the richest source of *Omega-3*. In many recipes that call for one particular species of fish, suggestions for substitutions have been provided.

DIPS AND SAUCES

●

• FAST SALSA

2 cups fresh tomatoes, diced
½ cup yellow or purple onion, finely diced
¼ cup cilantro, finely chopped
2–3 serrano chilies, deveined, seeds removed, and finely diced (dice as is with seeds for a hotter salsa)
½ clove garlic, finely minced or crushed
2 tablespoons lemon juice
½ teaspoon salt (a must)

Mix the diced tomatoes, onion, cilantro, and chilies. Stir in the garlic and lemon juice. Salt and toss. This is commonly served as a side dish. You may add it to spice up rice or to season fish, or use it as a "quick dip" with pita bread or raw vegetables.

Note: The serrano is one of the hotter varieties of chilies. It is a small deep-green chili, far smaller than its more common cousin, the jalapeño.

MAKES 1 CUP.
5 CALORIES PER TABLESPOON.

• Black Bean Dip

1 cup black beans
2 quarts water
1 bay leaf (optional)
⅓ cup plain yogurt
2 teaspoons Fast Salsa (see page 147)
½ teaspoon pepper, freshly ground

Place the black beans in the water and cook approximately 4 hours over medium heat. You may add a bay leaf while cooking to give these beans a very special taste. Drain the beans and reserve the cooking liquid. Add the beans to a blender or food processor with the remaining ingredients. Add the reserved bean liquid as needed to achieve a thick puree. Serve as a side dish with pita bread or as an appetizer with crudités, such as carrot sticks, cauliflower or broccoli flowerets, celery sticks, zucchini spears, or cherry tomatoes.

Makes 1 Cup.
16 Calories per Tablespoon.

• Curry Dip

1 cup low-calorie sour cream
½ clove garlic, minced
1 tablespoon fresh parsley, finely chopped (or ½ tablespoon dried)
1 tablespoon lemon juice
¼ teaspoon paprika
½ teaspoon curry powder (may need to increase to desired taste)
¼ teaspoon horseradish

Mix together all the ingredients. Chill. This is excellent as a party dip served with raw crudités.

Makes 1 Cup.
16 Calories per Tablespoon.

• Mexican Bean Dip

2 cups pinto beans
3 quarts water
2–3 ounces canned green chilies, chopped
¼ cup cilantro, finely chopped
1 onion, finely diced
1 teaspoon chili powder
¼ teaspoon cumin

Rinse the pinto beans and place in the water. Cook over medium heat until soft, about 4 hours. Drain, reserving the broth for later use. Place the beans in a blender and add the rest of the ingredients. Add the reserved broth as needed to achieve a smooth puree. Serve as a side dish with pita bread or as an appetizer with crudités.

Makes 1 Cup.
22 Calories per Tablespoon.

• Hot Artichoke-Chili Dip

1 (8–12-ounce) can artichoke hearts, drained
1 (4-ounce) can green chilies, finely chopped
4 ounces low-fat cheddar cheese, grated

Place the artichoke hearts in a food processor and blend until smooth. Mix the chilies and cheese into the artichoke puree. Place in small crocks. Freeze any that you won't be using.

To serve, preheat the oven to 350°F and heat through for 5 to 10 minutes, or microwave 1 minute until the cheese melts. Serve with raw crudités or whole-grain crackers, tortilla chips, or pita bread.

Makes 1½ Cups.
15 Calories per Tablespoon.

• YOGURT-SHALLOT SAUCE

1 cup low-fat yogurt (or 1 cup nonfat yogurt, recipe on page 98)
2 shallots (about 3 tablespoons), finely chopped (or 3–4 fresh chives, finely chopped)
2 tablespoons fresh parsley, minced (or 1 tablespoon dried parsley)
salt and pepper to taste

Mix together the yogurt, shallots, parsley, salt, and pepper. Cover and chill until serving time. Serve as a side dish to accompany fish or as an appetizer with cucumber sticks or cherry tomatoes.

MAKES 1 CUP.
12 CALORIES PER TABLESPOON.

• YOGURT-CILANTRO SAUCE

½ cup low-fat yogurt (or 1 cup nonfat yogurt, recipe on page 98)
3 tablespoons cilantro, finely chopped
¼ teaspoon ground cumin
¼ teaspoon garlic salt
Tabasco

Mix together the yogurt, cilantro, cumin, garlic salt, and Tabasco. Turn into a small bowl, cover, and chill for 30 minutes or longer.

MAKES ½ CUP.
10 CALORIES PER TABLESPOON.

• TARTAR SAUCE

¼ cup bell pepper, coarsely chopped
¼ cup yellow onion, coarsely chopped
1½ teaspoons red wine vinegar
¼ teaspoon dry mustard
¼ teaspoon cream of tartar
1 tablespoon lemon juice
1 cup low-calorie sour cream

Place all the ingredients in a blender, and blend until smooth. Place in the refrigerator to chill and thicken for at least 2 hours.

MAKES 1 PINT.
18 CALORIES PER TABLESPOON.

• ITALIAN TOMATO SAUCE

¾ cup onion, chopped
1 clove garlic, minced
1 tablespoon olive oil
4 pounds tomatoes, peeled and quartered
1 (6-ounce) can tomato paste
½ cup water
1 dried bay leaf
1 teaspoon basil
½ teaspoon oregano

In a large saucepan, sauté the onion and garlic in olive oil until the onion is soft. Add the tomatoes, tomato paste, water, and bay leaf. Simmer very slowly, uncovered, for 1½ hours, or until the sauce is thick. Stir occasionally. Add the basil and oregano, and simmer 20 minutes longer.

MAKES 4 CUPS.
12 CALORIES PER TABLESPOON.

SIDE DISHES

───────────────────●───────────────────

• OVEN-FRIED POTATOES

4 medium-sized russet potatoes
1 tablespoon dried spice of choice (tarragon, curry, paprika, or chili powder)

Preheat the oven to 350°F. Bake the potatoes for 45 minutes, until cooked. Allow to cool; you may store them in the refrigerator for use later in the week.

Preheat the oven to 350°F. Slice the cooked potatoes lengthwise like french fries or into thin wedges or round slices for "cottage-style" fries. Place the potatoes on a nonstick baking sheet and season with a spice of choice. "Dry-fry" in the oven for 15 minutes on each side, or until golden brown.

SERVES 4.
100 CALORIES PER POTATO.

• MINESTRONE

3 chicken bouillon cubes
3 cups water
3 cups tomato juice
1 cup onion, finely chopped
1 clove garlic, finely minced or crushed
¼ teaspoon marjoram
½ teaspoon basil
½ teaspoon oregano
2 ounces elbow macaroni, either semolina or whole wheat
2 zucchini
1 potato
4 carrots
½ green cabbage, shredded
½ cup canned kidney beans
¼ cup Parmesan cheese, grated

Combine the bouillon, water, tomato juice, onion, garlic, marjoram, basil, and oregano in a soup kettle and bring to a boil. Add the macaroni and vegetables to the soup and simmer until tender, about 20 minutes. Add the kidney beans and mix well. Sprinkle with Parmesan cheese and serve.

MAKES 4 CUPS.
100 CALORIES PER CUP.

• BROWN RICE AND VEGETABLES

2 cups canned chicken broth (or chicken bouillon)
1 cup brown rice, washed
¼ cup onion, chopped
¼ cup bell pepper, chopped
½ cup celery, chopped
½ cup mushrooms, chopped
1 teaspoon thyme
4 tablespoons dried parsley, finely chopped (or 2 tablespoons fresh parsley)

Pour the chicken stock in a saucepan with a tight lid and boil. Slowly add the rice to the boiling stock, reduce heat, cover, and simmer for 1 hour. Remove from the heat.

Preheat the oven to 350°F. Stir the vegetables and thyme into the rice mixture and place in an ovenproof baking dish. Bake for 30 minutes. Remove from the oven and serve sprinkled with parsley.

SERVES 4.
20 CALORIES PER ½ CUP.

• CAULIFLOWER AND PEAS IN YOGURT

2 quarts water
1 medium-sized head cauliflower, cut into flowerets
1 cup canned green peas, drained
¼ teaspoon cumin
⅛ teaspoon pepper, freshly ground
1 tablespoon lemon juice
3 tablespoons cilantro, finely chopped
¾ cup yogurt
salt to taste

Bring the water to a boil and add the cauliflower flowerets; boil for about 10 minutes until tender. Drain and place in a serving dish. Mix in the rest of the ingredients. Place in the refrigerator until chilled. Serve cool.

SERVES 4.
87 CALORIES PER SERVING.

• CURRY RICE

2 cups water
1 cup brown rice
1 apple, cored and peeled, finely diced
1–2 tablespoons curry

Bring the water to a boil. Add the brown rice and return to a boil. Add the apple and curry. Stir well. Add more curry if desired. Simmer covered for 45 minutes.

SERVES 4.
131 CALORIES PER SERVING.

• ZUCCHINI WITH APPLES

1½ tablespoons margarine
½ cup onion, finely chopped
1 pound zucchini, trimmed but not peeled, cut into ½-inch slices
1 cup tomatoes, peeled and chopped
salt to taste
¼ teaspoon pepper, freshly ground
1 cup apples, cored, peeled, and diced
½ teaspoon basil
2 tablespoons fresh parsley, finely chopped (or 1 tablespoon dried parsley)

Place the margarine in a large pan on top of the stove over low heat. Add the onion and sauté until soft. Add the zucchini, tomatoes, salt, and pepper. Mix gently. Cover and simmer slowly for 10 minutes. Add the apples and basil. Simmer covered for 5 minutes more. Uncover; turn the apples and zucchini, and cook approximately 5 minutes longer, or until zucchini is tender. Garnish with parsley before serving.

SERVES 4.
90 CALORIES PER SERVING.

FISH MAIN COURSES

———————————————•———————————————

• OVEN-FRIED FILLETS

2 pounds fish fillets (red snapper, fillet of sole, halibut)
¼ cup low-fat milk
1 cup bread crumbs mixed with paprika
2 tablespoons olive oil
parsley (for garnish)
lemon wedges (for garnish)

When you want to achieve the results of deep-fat frying, but you don't want the fat, try a technique called oven-frying. This method is most adaptable to the firmer types of fillets and for smaller fish that are usually fried whole.

Preheat the oven to 450°F. Dip the fish fillets in milk; then roll the fillets in bread crumbs. Place the fish in an oiled baking dish. Brush the fish with the olive oil. Bake about 20 minutes, or until crispy. Garnish with parsley and lemon.

SERVES 4.
390 CALORIES PER SERVING.

• MACKEREL GRILLED WITH BUTTERMILK

¾ cup buttermilk
2 large whole mackerels, to equal 2 pounds
1 tablespoon Parmesan cheese, grated
1 tablespoon parsley
1 tablespoon dill
1 tablespoon fennel
2 teaspoons pepper, freshly ground

Preheat the oven to 450°F. Pour the buttermilk into a baking dish large enough to hold the fish in one layer. Place the fish in the dish skin side down. Mix the cheese, herbs, and ground pepper together and sprinkle over the fish. Turn the oven heat to broil and place the baking dish 4 to 5 inches from the heat source. Grill for 10 minutes, occasionally basting with the liquid to prevent burning.

SERVES 4.
423 CALORIES PER SERVING.

• SALMON RISOTTO

3 cups canned chicken broth (or chicken bouillon)
½ cup dry white wine
2 tablespoons butter, sweet unsalted
¼ cup onion, finely chopped
1 cup short-grain rice
¼ pound salmon or lox, finely chopped
⅓ cup Parmesan cheese, freshly grated, if possible
black pepper, freshly ground to taste

This is a great way to turn a small amount of leftover salmon or smoked salmon (lox) into a dish fit for a gourmet.

Combine the chicken broth and wine in a saucepan; bring to a boil. Reduce the heat and simmer the liquid slowly to reduce to 2½ cups. In a skillet, melt the butter and sauté the onion until transparent. Add the rice, stirring for 2 minutes to coat the rice well with the onion and butter. Add a half cup of the liquid to the rice mixture, cook, stirring continually until the liquid is absorbed. Add another half cup of the liquid; continue cooking and stirring for several minutes until the liquid is absorbed. Add the salmon and another half cup of the liquid, and continue cooking and stirring, adding the remaining liquid as previous liquid is absorbed. Be careful that the liquid does not completely evaporate, or the risotto will burn. The mixture is ready when the rice is soft but still slightly chewy. While still hot, stir in the Parmesan cheese and pepper to taste. Gently toss with a fork and serve immediately.

SERVES 4.
280 CALORIES PER SERVING.

• RED SNAPPER IN FOIL

½ cup nonfat plain yogurt
½ teaspoon cumin
2 pounds red snapper, cut to make 4 fillets
1 cup Fast Salsa (see page 147)
8 whole sprigs cilantro (for garnish)
1 lime, thinly sliced (for garnish)

Preheat the oven to 450°F. Combine the yogurt and cumin. Add the fish to the marinade. Allow to sit at room temperature for 1 hour. Place the marinated fish in aluminum foil and top with salsa. Fold the foil over the fish to seal tightly. Bake for 10 minutes. Remove the cooked fish from the foil and place on a serving dish. Garnish with cilantro sprigs and lime slices.

SERVES 4.
415 CALORIES PER SERVING.

• TUNA CREOLE

2 medium onions, finely chopped
2 medium green peppers, finely chopped
1 tablespoon butter, sweet unsalted
1 tablespoon olive oil
3 tomatoes, peeled and finely chopped (see page 109 for preparation)
1 cup water
2 cups canned chicken broth (or chicken bouillon)
1 bay leaf
1 teaspoon thyme
1 tablespoon white pepper
1 tablespoon cayenne pepper
1 tablespoon black pepper, freshly ground
2 pounds fresh tuna, cut into 1-inch cubes

Sauté the onion and green pepper in butter and olive oil for about 4 minutes. Add the tomatoes, water, chicken stock, bay leaf, thyme, and 3 different kinds of pepper. Bring to a boil; cover and simmer for 45 minutes. Add the tuna cubes and simmer another 10 minutes. Serve with steamed white rice.

SERVES 4.
400 CALORIES PER SERVING.

• FISH 'N' POTATO HASH

1 tablespoon olive oil or corn oil
½ cup green onion, finely chopped
3 cups baked potatoes, peeled and diced
2 cups cooked, flaked white fish, salmon or tuna (may substitute canned, drained)
1 tablespoon Worcestershire sauce
¼ teaspoon cayenne pepper
1 teaspoon salt
1 teaspoon black pepper, freshly ground
2 tablespoons cilantro, finely chopped

This is an excellent way to use leftover baked potatoes.

Place the oil in a saucepan. Add the onion and sauté over medium heat until just limp. Add the potatoes and stir well with the onion. Sauté over low heat for 4 to 5 minutes. Add the flaked fish, blend well, and add Worcestershire sauce, cayenne pepper, salt, and pepper. Press down in the pan with a spatula and cook for 10 to 15 minutes, or until the hash is crusty on the bottom. Remove the hash to a serving dish, sprinkle with chopped cilantro, and serve.

Note: The potatoes may be baked in a 350°F oven for 45 minutes, then cooled, peeled, and diced. You may bake them a day ahead of time or simply use leftover baked potatoes.

SERVES 4.
415 CALORIES PER SERVING.

• GRILLED TROUT

½ cup soy sauce
½ cup sherry
1 tablespoon lemon rind, finely grated
1 clove garlic, crushed
4 whole trout
¼ lemon wedge
1 teaspoon basil
1 teaspoon oregano

Blend the soy sauce, sherry, lemon rind, and garlic. Brush the trout with the juice from the lemon wedge and sprinkle with the basil and oregano. Place in a shallow pan and pour on the marinade. Let stand 1 hour in the refrigerator, turning once.

Place the trout skin side down on aluminum foil under the broiler about 3 to 5 inches from the heat source and broil for about 3 to 5 minutes. Baste with the leftover marinade and serve.

SERVES 4.
440 CALORIES PER SERVING.

• HONG KONG SHRIMP

1 pound (about 16) shelled fresh shrimp (or deveined frozen shrimp)
2 tablespoons dried salted black beans (may substitute soy sauce)
1 small clove garlic, crushed
1 tablespoon ginger root, freshly ground
2 tablespoons corn oil
1 teaspoon salt (optional)
1¼ cups water

For Gravy:
½ cup water
2 tablespoons cornstarch
2 tablespoons oyster sauce
2 green onions, finely chopped

Slit the shrimp on the back side about halfway into the shrimp from head to tail. Devein and rinse the shrimp. Drain and set aside. Rinse the black beans in cool water, rinsing away most of the black skin of the beans. Combine the garlic, ginger root, and black beans and mix thoroughly. Place in a bowl and set aside.

In a wok or skillet heat the corn oil. Add the salt to the hot oil. Sauté the shrimp in hot oil for about 5 minutes, or until the shrimp turn pink; then add the black bean mixture, stirring constantly. Add ¼ cup water and bring to a boil. Remove from heat and allow to cool for about 1 minute.

For gravy, mix ½ cup water, the cornstarch, and oyster sauce in a cup. Remove the shrimp to a separate dish, leaving the liquid in the pan. Return the wok or skillet to high heat. Add the cornstarch mixture and bring to a full boil, stirring constantly. Once the liquid comes to full boil, quickly drop the shrimp into the gravy mixture and toss thoroughly. Remove from heat. Add the chopped green onion and serve.

Note: Black beans and oyster sauce are available in the oriental food section of most supermarkets.

SERVES 4.
180 CALORIES PER SERVING.

• HALIBUT STEAKS WITH SHALLOTS AND BASIL

4 8-ounce halibut steaks
2 tablespoons shallots, minced
2 tablespoons butter, sweet unsalted
1 tablespoon lemon juice
¼ teaspoon salt
¼ teaspoon pepper, freshly ground
4 tablespoons basil, finely chopped

Sauté the steaks in a nonstick skillet over medium heat for 4 to 5 minutes per side. In a saucepan, sauté the shallots in 1 tablespoon butter over medium heat for 2 to 3 minutes. When the ingredients are completely blended, over low heat, slowly whisk in the remaining butter. Add the lemon juice. Season the sauce with the salt and pepper, or to taste. When ready to serve, stir in the basil and spoon the sauce over the halibut on a serving platter.

Note: Good substitutes for halibut are salmon, shark, and tuna.

SERVES 4.
454 CALORIES PER SERVING.

• SALMON STEAKS WITH LEMON SAUCE

¾ cup lemon juice
1 tablespoon butter, sweet unsalted
2 tablespoons onion, finely minced
½ teaspoon salt (optional)
¼ teaspoon pepper, freshly ground
1½ tablespoons light brown sugar
1 teaspoon dry mustard
4 salmon steaks
2 tablespoons fresh parsley, finely chopped

In a saucepan, combine the lemon juice, butter, onion, salt, pepper, brown sugar, and mustard. Bring to a boil. Place the salmon steaks in a shallow baking dish. Pour half the lemon juice mixture over the fish. Preheat the oven on broil. Broil about 15 minutes, turning once. Baste frequently with the remaining lemon sauce mixture. Sprinkle with the parsley and serve.

SERVES 4.
457 CALORIES PER SERVING.

• OREGON-STYLE SALMON STEAKS

1 teaspoon rosemary, finely crushed
2 tablespoons white vinegar
2 tablespoons corn oil
salt and pepper to taste
2 pounds salmon, cut to make 4 (2-inch) steaks
2 lemons or limes, cut into wedges

Combine the rosemary, vinegar, and corn oil, and let stand at room temperature 30 minutes to make a marinade. Pour over the salmon for at least 30 minutes (longer if desired). Preheat the oven on broil. Place the steaks in the broiler 2 inches from the heat; broil 5 to 8 minutes on each side, or until the fish flakes easily. Serve with the lemon or lime wedges.

SERVES 4.
460 CALORIES PER SERVING.

• SAUTÉED PRAWNS WITH GREENS

1 tablespoon cornstarch
2 tablespoons cold water
16 prawns or large shrimp, to make 1½ pounds
3 tablespoons corn oil
1 clove garlic, finely minced or crushed
1 tablespoon ginger, finely grated (or dried)
1 cup celery, thinly sliced
1 onion, sliced into thin wedges
3 stalks Chinese chard, cut into large pieces (may substitute regular chard)
1½ dozen snow peas (may substitute ¼ cup canned petite peas)
3 tablespoons sherry

Dissolve the cornstarch in the cold water and set aside. Remove the shells and devein the prawns or shrimp. Wash thoroughly; then dry on paper towels. Heat the oil in a wok or skillet until it bubbles. Add the prawns to the hot oil. Stir vigorously for a few seconds and add the garlic. Cook until the prawns turn pink. Remove the prawns from the heat. Add the ginger, celery, onion, chard, and snow peas to the hot skillet. Cook for 3 minutes. Return the prawns to the skillet with the vegetables. Add the sherry and water-cornstarch mixture to thicken. Cook for 2 minutes. Be careful not to overcook, as the prawns will become tough.

SERVES 4.
280 CALORIES PER SERVING.

• CIOPPINO

4 tablespoons olive oil
1 large onion, finely diced
1 green pepper, finely diced
3 cloves garlic, finely minced or crushed
⅓ cup fresh parsley, finely chopped
1 (8-ounce) can tomato puree
1 (8-ounce) can tomato sauce
2 cups water
1 teaspoon salt
¼ teaspoon pepper
½ pound shelled, cooked crab (may substitute canned crab meat)
1 pound small clams, washed and scrubbed
½ pound red snapper, cut into 1-inch cubes
½ pound shrimp and/or lobster
1 cup pale dry sherry

In a frying pan heat the oil over medium-high heat. Add the onion, green pepper, and garlic, stirring slowly for 5 minutes. In an 8-quart pot add the parsley, tomato puree, tomato sauce, water, salt, and pepper. Bring to a boil and add the sautéed onion, green pepper, and garlic. Reduce the heat; cover and simmer for 1 hour.

Meanwhile prepare the crab, clams, shrimp and/or lobster, and snapper. Add the clams to the sauce. Raise the heat when the sauce begins to boil and the first clam opens, add the snapper, shrimp and/or lobster. Cook for 3 minutes. Be careful to avoid overcooking. The last to be added are the cooked crab and the sherry. Simmer for 3 minutes.

SERVES 4.
500 CALORIES PER SERVING.

• CEVICHE

½ pound red snapper, cut in 1-inch cubes
½ pound shrimp or scallops
¼ cup lime juice (or juice of 1 lime)
1 cup peeled, seeded tomato, cut into ¼-inch cubes (see page 109)
4 canned serrano chilies
½ cup red onion, finely chopped
¼ cup celery, finely diced
¼ cup canned tomato sauce
1 tablespoon olive oil
1 tablespoon cilantro, finely chopped
½ teaspoon dried oregano
zest of 1 lime (grated rind)
½ teaspoon pepper, freshly ground

Place the red snapper and shrimp or scallops in a bowl. Add the lime juice. Cover and refrigerate, stirring occasionally, 12 hours, or let sit overnight to fully marinate. Add the tomato, chilies, onion, celery, tomato sauce, olive oil, cilantro, oregano, and lime peel. Season to taste with pepper. Chill.

SERVES 4.
180 CALORIES PER SERVING.

• BEAN AND TUNA SALAD

1 cup canned kidney beans, rinsed
1 cup canned garbanzo beans, rinsed
1 (7½-ounce) can water-packed white tuna
¼ cup rinsed capers, finely chopped
½ cup white onion, thinly sliced
¼ cup fresh parsley, finely chopped
1 large clove garlic, finely minced or crushed

Combine the beans, tuna, capers, onion, parsley, and garlic in a bowl, and toss to fully mix all the ingredients. Pour the Vinaigrette Dressing over the bean and tuna salad. Chill before serving.

SERVES 4.
412 CALORIES PER SERVING (INCLUDES DRESSING).

• VINAIGRETTE DRESSING

⅛ cup olive oil
½ cup red wine vinegar
1–2 tablespoons Dijon mustard
½ teaspoon salt
Freshly ground pepper to taste

In a separate bowl or glass jar add all the ingredients and mix or shake well.

• PAELLA

¼ cup olive oil
2 pounds fryer chicken, cut up and skin removed
½ teaspoon salt
½ teaspoon black pepper, freshly ground
1 small onion, finely diced
2 cloves garlic, crushed
1 bell pepper, cut into ¼-inch strips
2 cups long-grain rice
1 cup fresh tomatoes, peeled, seeded, and diced (see p. 109)
6 cups canned chicken broth (may substitute chicken bouillon)
1 dried bay leaf
½ teaspoon powdered saffron
12 medium clams, well scrubbed
8 large whole shrimp (unshelled)
1 cup frozen peas (may substitute cut-up string beans or asparagus)
1 teaspoon cayenne pepper (may substitute Tabasco sauce)
1 lemon, cut into wedges

Heat half of the olive oil in a large skillet. When the oil begins to smoke, add the chicken and season with salt and pepper while frying. When the chicken turns golden brown, remove from the pan and set aside. Add the remaining oil to the pan and sauté the onion, garlic, bay leaf, cayenne pepper, and pepper strips until light brown. Add the rice and stir until well coated with oil. Add the tomatoes and cook until the liquid evaporates. Stir frequently with a wooden spoon. Heat the chicken broth. Dissolve the saffron in 1 cup hot chicken broth and pour into the pan. Stir until the saffron blends with the rice. Now pour 2 cups of the boiling chicken broth over the rice. Cook over medium-high heat, stirring gently and continuously until the rice has absorbed the liquid. Once dry, add 2 more cups of the boiling chicken broth to the rice and stir continuously. Permit the rice to absorb the liquid while taking care not to allow the heat to burn the bottom of the rice. Remove from the heat.

Preheat the oven to 350°F. Return the chicken to the pan. Pour 2 cups of the hot chicken broth into the pan. Distribute the clams, shrimp, and peas throughout the Paella. Place the skillet in the oven for 20 minutes, or until all the liquid is absorbed. Garnish with lemon wedges and serve.

MAKES 6 TO 8 SERVINGS.
580 CALORIES PER SERVING.

Fish Calorie Chart

SPECIES	CALORIES (kcal)	OMEGA-3 (gm)
Anchovy	144	1.58
Barracuda, Pacific	134	-0-
Bass, black sea	109	-0-
Bass, striped	106	.8
Buffalo or sucker	244	-0-
Carp	166	.56
Catfish, freshwater	130	.68
Catfish, ocean, wollfish	114	.79
Cod, Atlantic	85	.22
Cod, Pacific	90	.11
American eel	253	1.36
Flounder, flatfish or sole	93	-0-
Flounder, yellowtail	106	.22
Haddock	94	.22
Halibut, Atlantic	130	1.47
Halibut, Pacific	119	.56
Herring	114	-0-

SPECIES	CALORIES (kcal)	OMEGA-3 (gm)
Herring, Atlantic	169	1.36
Herring, Pacific	183	1.36
Herring, Thread	127	.68
Mackerel	196	-0-
Mackerel, Atlantic	199	2.15
Mackerel, Pacific (chub)	146	1.24
Mahimahi, dolphin fish	101	-0-
Monkfish, goosefish, anglerfish	90	-0-
Mullet, striped	130	.45
Perch: Lake, yellow perch	97	.22
Perch: Ocean, redfish	119	.45
Pike, northern	98	.11
Pike, walleye		.22
Atlantic pompano	187	-0-
Rockfish	81	.34
Sablefish, black cod	208	1.47
Salmon, Atlantic	146	1.58
Salmon: Pacific Chinook, king	208	2.15
Salmon: Chum, keta	141	.68
Salmon: Silver Coho	170	1.7
Salmon, pink, humpback	148	1.7
Salmon: Sockeye	179	3.06
Spanish Sardine	150	1.36
Shark: Spiny dogfish	189	2.15
Smelt	111	.68
Red snapper	124	.68
Sole	99	.11
Sole, Dover (Pacific)	82	-0-
Sole, Petrale	104	-0-
Sole, Rex	86	-0-
Sole, Rock	99	-0-
Atlantic sturgeon	111	.22
Swordfish	138	1.02
Trout, Rainbow	148	1.24
Trout, Brook	122	.34
Trout, Lake	183	1.58
Tuna: Albacore or longfin	195	2.38

(Figures are percentages)

1% or less fat
Cod, Atlantic and Pacific
Haddock
Northern pike
Blue shark
Mahimahi
Yellow perch   1.0
Rockfish   1.0

5% or less fat
Snapper   1.1
Flounder   1.2
Walleye   1.4
Monkfish   1.5
Atlantic croaker   1.7
Pacific pompano   2.0
Smelt   2.1
Striped bass   2.2
Pacific halibut   2.2
Yellowfin tuna   2.5
Brook trout   2.5
Skipjack tuna   2.7
Ocean perch   2.8
Bluefish   2.9
Barracuda   3.1
Atlantic sturgeon   3.2
Atlantic halibut   3.6
Sea catfish   3.6
Chum salmon   4.2
Swordfish   4.4
Channel catfish   4.4
Pacific mackerel   4.8
Anchovy   4.8
Pink salmon   5.0

10% or less fat

Bonito	5.5
Atlantic salmon	5.6
Rainbow trout	5.8
Spanish mackerel	5.9
Bluefin tuna	6.1
Cisco	6.4
Coho salmon	6.6
Sardine	6.8
Albacore tuna	7.2
Sockeye salmon	7.9
Atlantic herring	8.0
Carp	8.5
Whitefish	9.0
Lake trout	9.4
Pompano	9.5
Pacific herring	9.8

More than 10% fat

Atlantic mackerel	10.7
Lake sturgeon	10.8
Butterfish	11.2
King salmon	11.4
Shad	12.5
Sablefish	14.2
American eel	15.8
Buffalo	16.6
Sirloin steak	27.0

Bibliography

AHMED, A.A., AND HOLUB, B. J. "Alteration and Recovery of Bleeding Times, Platelet Aggregation and Fatty Acid Composition of Individual Phospholipids in Plateles of Human Subjects Receiving Cod Liver Oil." *Lipids* 19(8) (1984): 617–24.

ARNTZENIUS, A.C., ET AL. "Diet, Lipoproteins, and the Progression of Coronary Atherosclerosis—The Leiden Intervention Trial." *New England Journal of Medicine* 312(1985): 805.

ARTHAUD, B. "Cause of Death in 339 Alaskan Natives as Determined by Autopsy." *A.M.A. Archives of Pathology* 90(1970): 433–38.

BANG, H.O., AND DYERBERG, J. "The Bleeding Tendency in Greenland Eskimos." *Danish Medical Bulletin* 27(1980): 202–205.

BANG, H.O., ET AL. "Plasmalipid and Lipoproteins Patterns in Greenland West Coast Eskimos." *Lancet* i(1971):1143–46.

———. "Composition of Food Consumed by Greenland Eskimos." *Acta Medica Scandinavia* 200(1976): 69–73.

BATES, C., ET AL. "Plasma Essential Fatty Acids in Pure and Mixed Race American Indians On and Off a Diet Exceptionally Rich in Salmon." *Prostaglandins, Leukotrienes & Medicine* 17(1)(1985): 77–84.

BEGIN, M.E., ET AL. "Selective Killing of Human Cancer Cells by Polyunsaturated Fatty Acids." *Prostaglandins, Leukotrienes & Medicine* 19(2)(1985): 117–86.

BLACK, K.L., ET AL. "EPA: Effect on Brain Prostaglandins, Cerebral Blood Flow and Edema in Ischemic Gembrils." *Stroke* 15(1984): 65.

BLANKENHORN, D.H. "Two New Diet-Heart Studies." *New England Journal of Medicine* 312(1985): 851.

BOBERG, M., ET AL. "Fatty Acid Composition of Platelets and of Plasma Lipid Esters in Relation to Platelet Function in Patients with Ischaemic Heart Disease." *Atherosclerosis* 58(1985): 49–63.

BOOYENS, J., ET AL. "Chronic Arachidonic Acid Eicosanoid Imbalance: A Common Feature in Coronary Artery Disease, Hypercholesterolemia, Cancer and Other Important Diseases Significance of Desaturase Enzyme Inhibition of the Arachidonic Acid Desaturase-Independent Pathway." *Medical Hypotheses* 18(1)(1985): 53–60.

———— "Dietary Fats and Cancer." *Medical Hypotheses* 17(1985): 351–62.

BRENSIKE, J.F., ET AL. "Effects of Therapy with Cholestyramine on Progression of Coronary Arteriosclerosis: Results of the NHLBI Type II Coronary Intervention Study." *Circulation* 69(2)(1984): 313–24.

BRESALIER, R.S., AND KIM, Y.S. "Diet and Colon Cancer." *New England Journal of Medicine* 313(1985): 1413–14.

BRONSGEEST-SCHOUTE, H.C., ET AL. "The Effect of Various Intakes of w-3 Fatty Acids on the Blood Lipid Composition in Healthy Human Subjects." *American Journal of Clinical Nutrition* 34(1981): 1752–57.

BROWN, M., ET AL. "The Occurrence of Cancer in an Eskimo." *Cancer* 5(1952): 142–43.

BROX, J.H., ET AL. "Effects of Cod Liver Oil on Platelets and Coagulation in Familial Hypercholesterolemia (Type IIa)." *Acta Medica Scandinavia* 213(1983): 137–44.

BROX, J.H., AND NORDOY, A. "The Effect of Polyunsaturated Fatty Acids on Endothelial Cells and Their Production of Prostacyclin; Thromboxane and Platelet Inhibitory Activity." *Thrombosis Haemostasis* 50(4)(1983): 762–67.

BUCHVALD, H., ET AL. "Overview of Randomized Clinical Trials of Lipid Intervention for Atherosclerotic Cardiovascular Disease." *Controlled Clinical Trials* 3(1982): 271.

CASALIO, R.E., ET AL. "Improved Graft Patency Associated with Altered Platelet Function Induced by Marine Fatty Acids in Dogs." *Journal of Surgical Research* 40(1)(1986): 6–12.

CONNOR, W.E. "Polyunsaturated Fatty Acids, Hyperlipedemia, and Thrombosis." *Arteriosclerosis* 2(1982): 87–113.

CONNER, W.E., AND CONNER, S.L. "The Key Role of Nutritional Factors in the Prevention of Coronary Heart Disease." *Preventative Medicine* 1(1972): 49.

———. "Dietary Therapy of Hyperlipidemia." *Medical Clinics of North America* 66(2)(1982): 485.

CORCORAN, A.C., AND RABINOWITCH, I.M. "A Study of the Blood Lipids and Blood Protein in Canadian Eastern Arctic Eskimos." *Biochemical Journal* 31(1937): 543–48.

———. "Critique of Low Carbohydrate Ketogenic Weight Reduction Regimens, a Review of Dr. Atkins' Diet Revolution, Statement of the American Medical Council on Food and Nutrition." *J.A.M.A.* 224(1973): 1445.

CULP, B.R., ET AL. "Inhibition of Prostaglandin Biosynthesis by Eicosapentaenoic Acid." *Prostaglandin Medicine* 3(1979): 269.

———. "The Effect of Dietary Supplementation of Fish Oil on Experimental Myocardial Infarction." *Prostaglandins* 20(1980): 1021–31.

CUMMINGS, J. "Nutritional Implications of Dietary Fiber." *American Journal of Clinical Nutrition* 31(1978): 521.

DUFFIELD, R.G.M., ET AL. "Treatment of Hyperlipedemia Retards Progression of Symptomatic Femoral Atherosclerosis." *Lancet* ii(1983): 639.

DUSHECK, J. "Fish, Fatty Acids, and Physiology." *Science News* 128(1985): 252–54.

DYERBERG, J. AND BANG, H.O. "Haemostatic Function and Platelet Polyunsaturated Fatty Acids in Eskimos." *Lancet* ii(1979): 433–35.

DYERBERG, J., ET AL. "Fatty Acid Composition of the Plasma Lipids in Greenland Eskimos." *American Journal of Clinical Nutrition* 28(1975): 958–66.

———. "Plasma Cholesterol Concentration in Caucasian Danes and Greenland West Coast Eskimos." *Danish Medical Bulletin* 24(1977): 52–55.

———. "Dietary Fat and Thrombosis." *Lancet* i(1978): 152.

———. "EPA and Prevention of Thrombosis and Atherosclerosis." *Lancet* ii(1978): 117–19.

EATON, S.B., AND KONNER, M. "Paleolithic Nutrition." *New England Journal of Medicine* 312(1985): 283.

ENHORN, D.L.H., ET AL. "Eskimos and Their Diets." *Lancet* i(1983): 1335.

ENOS, W.F., ET AL. "Coronary Disease Among U.S. Soldiers Killed in Action in Korea." *J.A.M.A.* 152(1953): 1090–93.

————. "Eskimo Diets and Diseases." *Lancet* ii(1983): 1139–41.

FELDMAN, S.A., ET AL. "Lipid and Cholesterol Metabolism in Alaskan Arctic Eskimos." *A.M.A. Archives of Pathology* 94(1972): 42–58.

FISCHER, S., ET AL. "Prostaglandin 13 Is Formed in Vivo in Man after Dietary Eicosapentaenoic Acid." *Nature* 307(5947)(1984): 165–68.

FRIES, E. "Salt, Volume, and the Prevention of Hypertension." *Circulation* 53(1976): 589.

GARCIA-PALMIERI, M.R., ET AL. "Relationship of Dietary Intake to Subsequent Coronary Heart Disease Incidence: The Puerto Rico Heart Health Program." *American Journal of Clinical Nutrition* 33(1980): 1818–27.

GLOMSET, J.A. "Fish, Fatty Acids, and Human Health." *New England Journal of Medicine* 312(1985): 1253–54.

GOODNIGHT, S.H. JR., ET AL. "The Effects of Dietary Omega 3 Fatty Acids on Platelet Composition and Function in Man: A Prospective, Controlled Study." *Blood* 58(5)(1981): 880–85.

GORDON, T., ET AL. "High Density Lipoprotein as a Protective Factor Against Coronary Heart Disease. The Framingham Study." *American Journal of Medicine* 62(1977): 707–14.

————. "Diet and Its Relation to Coronary Heart Disease and Death in Three Populations." *Circulation* 63(1981): 500–15.

GOTTMAN, A.W. "A Report of 103 Autopsies on Alaskan Natives." *A.M.A. Archives of Pathology* 70(1960): 117–24.

GOTTO, A.M., ET AL. "Recommendations for Treatment of Hyperlipidemia in Adults: The Nutrition Committee and Council on Atherosclerosis of the American Heart Association." *Circulation* 69(1984): 1067A–90A.

GRUNDY, S.M., ET AL. "Rationale of the Diet-Heart Statement of the American Heart Association: Report of Nutrition Committee." *Circulation* 65(1982): 389A.

HADJIAGAPIOU, C., ET AL. "Eicosapentaenoic Acid Utilization by Bovine Aortic Endothelial Cells: Effects on Prostacyclin Production." *Biochimica Biophysics Acta* 875(2)(1986): 369–81.

HAFT, J. "Role of Platelets in Coronary Artery Disease." *American Journal of Cardiology* 43(1979): 1197.

HAMAZAKI, T., ET AL. "Effects of Fish Oil Rich in EPA on Serum Lipid in Hyperlipedemic Hemodialysis Patients." *Kidney International* 26(1)(1984): 81–84.

HAMBERG, M., ET AL. "Thromboxanes: A New Group of Biologically Active Compounds Derived from Prostaglandin Endoperoxides." *Proceedings of the National Academy of Science, U.S.A.* 72(1975): 2994–98.

HARRIS, W.S., ET AL. "Dietary Fish Oils, Plasmalipids and Platelets in Man." *Progress in Lipid Research* 20(1982): 75–79.

———. "Comparative Reductions of the Plasma Lipids and Lipoproteins by Dietary Polyunsaturated Fats: Salmon Oil vs. Vegetable Oil." *Metabolism* 32(1983): 179–84.

HAY, C., ET AL. "Effects of Fish Oil on Platelet Kinetics in Patients with Ischaemic Heart Disease." *Lancet* i(1982): 1269.

HEGSTED, D.M., ET AL. "Quantitative Effects of Dietary Fat on Serum Cholesterol." *American Journal of Clinical Nutrition* 17(1965): 281.

HENNING, B., ET AL. "Exposure to Fatty Acid Increases Human LDL Transfer Across Cultured Endothelial Monolayers." *Circulation Research* 57(5)(1985): 776–80.

HEROLD, P.M., AND KINSELLA, J.E. "Fish Oil Consumption and Decreased Risk of Cardiovascular Disease: A Comparison of Findings from Animal and Human Feeding Trials." *American Journal of Clinical Nutrition* 43(1986): 566.

HIRAI, A., ET AL. "EPA and Platelet Function in Japanese." *Lancet* ii(1980): 1132.

———. "Effects of the Oral Administration of Fish Oil Concentrate on the Release and the Metabolism of Arachidonic Acid and EPA by Human Platelets." *Thrombosis Research* 28(1982): 285.

HOEG, J.M., ET AL. "An Approach to the Management of Hyperlipoproteinemia." *J.A.M.A.* 255(1986): 512–21.

HOLMAN, R.T. *Lipids.* Volume 1. New York: Raven Press, 1976.

HORNSTRA, G. *Developments in Haematology and Immunology.* Volume 4. The Hague: Martinus Nijhoff Publishing, 1982.

HORNSTRA, G., ET AL. "Influence of Dietary Fat on Platelet Function in Man." *Lancet* i(1973): 1155.

————. "Fish Oil Feeding Lowers Thromboxane and Prostacyclin Production by Rat Platelets and Aorta and Does Not Result in the Formation of Prostaglandin I." *Prostaglandins* 21(1981): 727–38.

HORNSTRA, G., AND HEMKER, H.C. "Clot-Promoting Effect of Platelet-Vessel Wall Interactions: Influence of Dietary Fats and Relation to Arterial Thrombus Formation in Rats." *Haemostasis* 8(1979): 211.

ILLINGWORTH, R.D., ET AL. "Inhibitions of LDL Synthesis by Dietary Omega-3 Fatty Acids in Humans." *Arteriosclerosis* 4(1984): 270–75.

JOOSSENS, J. "Salt Intake and Mortality from Strokes." *New England Journal of Medicine* 300(1979): 1396.

JORGENSEN, K.A., AND DYERBERG, J. "Platelets and Atherosclerosis." *Advances in Nutritional Research* 5(1983): 57–75.

KAGAVA, Y., ET AL. "Eicosapolyenoic Acids of Serum Lipids of Japanese Islanders with Low Incidence of Cardiovascular Diseases." *Journal of Nutritional Science and Vitaminology* 28(1982): 441.

KANNEL, W. "Cholesterol in the Prediction of Atherosclerotic Disease." *American Internal Medicine* 90(1979): 85.

KANNEL, W.B. "Serum Cholesterol, Lipoproteins, and the Risk of Coronary Heart Disease: The Framingham Study." *American Internal Medicine* 74(1971): 1–11.

KEYS, A. "Coronary Heart Disease in Seven Countries." *Circulation* 41(suppl)(1970): 1–211.

————. *Seven Countries: A Multivariate Analysis of Death and Coronary Heart Disease.* Massachusetts: Harvard University Press, 1980.

KIFER, R.R., ET AL. "Effect of Dietary Fish Oil on the Fatty Acid Composition and Palatability of Pig Tissues." *Fishery Bulletin* 69(1971): 281–302.

KIRBY, R.W., ET AL. "Oat-Bran Intake Selectively Lowers Serum Low-Density Lipoprotein Cholesterol Concentrations of Hypercholesterolemic Men." *American Journal of Clinical Nutrition* 34(1981): 824–29.

KNAPP, H.R., ET AL. "Invivo Indexes of Platelet and Vascular Function During Fish Oil Administration in Patients with Atherosclerosis." *New England Journal of Medicine* 314(15)(1986): 937.

KNAPP, H.R., AND FITZGERALD, G.A. "Dietary Eicosapentaenoic Acid and Human Atherosclerosis." *Atherosclerosis Review* 13(1985): 127–43.

KOBAYASHI, S., ET AL. "Reduction of Blood Viscosity by Eicosapentaenoic Acid." *Lancet* ii(1981): 197.

KROGH, A., AND KROGH M. "A Study of the Diet and Metabolism of Eskimos Undertaken in 1908 on an Expedition to Greenland." *Medd Grenland* 51(1914): 1–2.

KROMHOUT, D., AND COULANDER, C.D.L. "Diet, Prevalence and 10-Year Mortality from Coronary Heart Disease in 871 Middle-Aged Men: The Zutphen Study." *American Journal of Epidemiology* 119(1984): 733–41.

KROMHOUT, D., ET AL. "Diet and 20-Year Mortality from Coronary Heart Disease." *New England Journal of Medicine* 312(1985): 811.

———. "The Inverse Relation Between Fish Consumption and 20-Year Mortality from Coronary Artery Disease." *New England Journal of Medicine* 312(1985): 1205–09.

LANDS, W.E.M., ET AL. "Relationship of Thromboxane Generation to the Aggregation and Platelets from Humans: Effects of EPA." *Prostaglandins.* 30(5)(1985): 819.

LANDYMORE, R., ET AL. "Cod-Liver Oil in the Prevention of Initial Hyperplasia in Autogenous Vein Grafts Used for Arterial Bypass." *Journal of Thoracic Cardiovascular Surgery* 89(3)(1985): 351–57.

LANDYMORE, R.W., ET AL. "Effects of Cod-Liver Oil on Intimal Hyperplasia in Vein Grafts Used for Arterial Bypass." *Canadian Journal of Surgery* 29(2)(1986): 129–31.

———. "Comparison of Cod-Liver and Aspirin-Dipyridamole for the Prevention of Intimal Hyperplasia in Autologous Vein Grafts." *Annals of Thoracic Surgery* 41(1)(1986): 54–57.

LEE, T.E., ET AL. "Effect of Dietary Enrichment with EPA and Docosahexaenoic Acid in Vitro Neutrophil and Monocyte Leukotriene Generation and Neutrophil Function." *New England Journal of Medicine* 312(1985): 1217–24.

———. "Lipid Research Clinics Coronary Prevention Trial Results: II. The Relationship of Reduction in Incidence of Coronary Heart Disease to Cholesterol Lowering." *J.A.M.A.* 24(1984): 365.

———. "Lipid Research Clinics Coronary Primary Prevention Trial Results: I. Reduction in Incidence of Coronary Heart Disease." *J.A.M.A.* 241(1984): 351.

LORENZ, R., ET AL. "Platelet Function, Thromboxane Formation and Blood Pressure Control During Supplementation of Western Diet with Cod Liver Oil." *Circulation* 67(3)(1983): 504–511.

MAIAURIE, J. *The Last Kings of Thule*. London: Jonathan Cape, 1982.

MCGEE, D.L., ET AL. "Ten-Year Incidence of Coronary Heart Disease in the Honolulu Heart Program: Relationship to Nutrient Intake." *American Journal of Epidemiology* 119(1984): 667–76.

MORGAN, T. "Hypertension Treated by Salt Restriction." *Lancet* i(1978): 227.

MORTENSEN, J.Z., ET AL. "Effect of N-6 and N-3 Polyunsaturated Fatty Acids on Haemostasis, Blood Lipids and Blood Pressure." *Thrombosis Haemostasis* 50(1983): 543–46.

———. "National Institutes of Health Consensus Conference on the Treatment of Hypertriglyceridemia." *J.A.M.A.* 251(1984): 1196–200.

———. "National Institutes of Health Consensus Development Conference Statement: Lowering Blood Cholesterol to Prevent Heart Disease." *J.A.M.A.* 253(1985): 2080–86.

NEEDLEMAN, P., ET AL. "Fatty Acids as Sources of Potential Magic Bullets for Modification of Platelet and Vascular Function." *Progress in Lipid Research* 20(1982): 415–422.

NELSON, A.M. "Diet Therapy in Coronary Disease—Effect on Mortality of High-Protein, High-Seafood, Fat-Controlled Diet." *Geriatrics* 27(1972): 103.

NESTEL, P. "Fish Oil Attenuates the Cholesterol Induced Rise in Lipoprotein Cholesterol." *American Journal of Clinical Nutrition* 43(1986): 752.

NESTEL, P.J., ET AL. "Suppression by Diets Rich in Fish Oil of VLDL Production in Man." *Journal of Clinical Investigation* 74(1)(1984): 82–89.

NORDOY, A. "Dietary Fatty Acids, Platelets, Endothelial Cells and Coronary Artery Disease." *Acta Medica Scandinavia* (Suppl.) 701(1985): 15.

NORELL, S.E., ET AL. "Fish Consumption and Mortality from Coronary Heart Disease." *British Medical Journal* 293(1986): 426.

NORRIS, P.G., ET AL. "Effect of Dietary Supplementation with Fish Oil on Systolic Blood Pressure in Mild Essential Hypertension." *British Medical Journal* 293(1986): 104–05.

PHILLIPSON, B.E., ET AL. "Reduction of Plasma Lipids, Lipoproteins, and Apoproteins by Dietary Fish Oils in Patients with Hypertriglyceridemia." *New England Journal of Medicine* 312(1985): 1210–16.

PITT, B., ET AL. "Prostaglandins and Prostaglandin Inhibitors in Ischemic Heart Disease." *Annals of Internal Medicine* 99(1983): 83.

PRESCOTT, S.M. "The Effect of EPA on Leukotriene B Production by Human Neutrophils." *Journal of Biological Chemistry* 259(12)(1984): 7615–21.

PUUSTINEN, T., ET AL. "Fatty Acid Composition of 12 North-European Fish Species." *Acta Medica Scandinavia* 218(1)(1985): 59–62.

ROBERTSON, T.L., ET AL. "Epidemiologic Studies of Coronary Disese and Stroke in Japanese Men; Living in Japan, Hawaii and California." *American Journal of Cardiology* 39(1977): 244.

RUITER, A., ET AL. "The Influence of Dietary Mackerel Oil on the Condition of Organs and on Blood Lipid Composition in the Young Growing Pig." *American Journal of Clinical Nutrition* 31(1978): 2159–66.

SANDER, T.A. "Dietary Fat and Platelet Function." *Clinical Science* 65(1983): 343–50.

SANDERS, T.A.B., AND ROSHANAI, F. "The influence of Different Types of w 3 Polyunsaturated Fatty Acids on Blood Lipids and Platelet Function in Healthy Volunteers." *Clinical Science* 64(1983): 91–99.

SANDERS, T., ET AL. "The Effect on Blood Lipids and Haemostasis of a Supplement of Cod Liver Oil, Rich in Eicosapentaenoic and Docosahexaenoic Acids, in Healthy Young Men." *Clinical Science* 61(1981): 317–24.

SCHIMKE, E., ET AL. "Influence of Cod Liver Oil Diet in Diabetics Type I on Fatty Acid Patterns and Platelet Aggregation." *Biomedica Biochimica Acta* 43(8–9) (1984): 5351–53.

SHEKELLE, R.B., ET AL. "Diet, Serum Cholesterol, and Death from Coronary Heart Disease: The Western Electric Study." *New England Journal of Medicine* 304(1981): 65–70.

———. "Fish Consumption and Mortality from Coronary Artery Disease." *New England Journal of Medicine* 313(1985): 820.

SIESS, W., ET AL. "Platelet Membrane Fatty Acids, Platelet Aggregation and Thromboxane Formation During a Mackerel Diet." *Lancet* i(1980):441–44.

SIMMONS, L.A., ET AL. "On the Effect of Dietary N-3 Fatty Acids on Plasma Lipids and Lipoproteins in Patients with Hyperlipidaemia." *Atherosclerosis* 54(1985): 75–88.

SINCLAIR, H.M. "The Diet of Canadian Indians and Eskimos." *Proceedings of the Nutrition Society* 12(1953): 69–82.

———. "Nutrition and Atherosclerosis." *Symposium of Zoological Society of London* 21(1968): 275–88.

————. "EPA and Platelet Function." *Twenty-third International Conference of Biochemical Problems & Lipids* 18(1981).

————. *Nahrung Aus Der Meer.* Berlin: Springer-Verlag, 1981.

————. *Nutrition and Killer Diseases.* New Jersey: Noyes, 1982.

SINGER, P., ET AL. "Lipid and Blood Pressure-Lowering Effect of Mackerel Diet in Man." *Atherosclerosis* 49(1)(1983): 99–108.

————. "Negative Correlation of EPA and Lipid Accumulation in Hepatocytes of Diabetics." *Biomedica Biochimica Acta* 43(8–9)(1984): 5438–42.

————. "Blood Pressure and Lipid-Lowering Effects of Mackerel and Herring Diet in Patients with Mild Essential Hypertension." *Atherosclerosis.* 56(2)(1985): 223–35.

STEFANSSON, V. *My Life with the Eskimo.* New York: Macmillan, 1913.

STEIN, M. "Ineffectiveness of Human Chorionic Gonadotropin in Weight Reduction." *American Journal of Nutrition* 29(1976): 940.

TERANO, T., ET AL. "Antiinflammatory Effects of Eicosapentaenoic Acid: Relevance to Icosanoid Formation." *Advances in Prostaglandin, Thromboxane and Leukotriene Research* 15(1985): 253–55.

THORNGREN, M., ET AL. "Effects of Acetylsalicylic Acid on Platelet Aggregation Before and During Increase in Dietary EPA." *Haemostasis* 13(4)(1983): 244–47.

————. "Plasma Lipoproteins and Fatty Acid Composition During a Moderate Eicosapentaenoic Acid Diet." *Acta Medica Scandinavia* 219(1)(1986): 23–28.

TUMURA, Y., ET AL. "Effects of Eicosapentaenoic Acid on Hemostatic Function and Serum Lipids in Humans." *Advances in Prostaglandin, Thromboxane and Leukotriene Research* 15(1985): 265–67.

VAS DIAS, F.W., ET AL. "The Effect of Polyunsaturated Fatty Acids of the n-3 and n-6 Series of Platelet Aggregation and Platelet and Aortic Fatty Acid Composition in Rabbits." *Atherosclerosis* 43(1982): 245–57.

VELICAN, E., AND VELICAN, C. "Atherosclerotic Involvement of the Coronary Arteries of Adolescents and Young Adults." *Atherosclerosis* 36(1980): 449.

VESSELINOVITCH, D., ET AL. "Reversal of Advanced Atherosclerosis in Rhesus Monkeys." *Atherosclerosis* 23(1976): 155.

VON LOSSONCZY, T.O., ET AL. "The Effect of a Fish Diet on Serum Lipids in Healthy Human Subjects." *American Journal of Clinical Nutrition* 31(1978):1340–46.

VONSHACKEY, C., AND WEBER, P. "Metabolism and Effects on Platelet Function of the Purified Eicosapentaenoic and Docosahexaenoic Acids in Humans." *Journal of Clinical Investigation* 76(6)(1985): 2446–50.

WEKSLER, B.B., ET AL. "Platelets and Atherosclerosis." *American Journal of Medicine* 71(1981): 331.

WISSLER, R.W. *Heart Disease: A Textbook of Cardiovascular Medicine.* Philadelphia: W.B. Saunders, 1980.

WOOKCOCK, B.E., ET AL. "Beneficial Effect of Fish Oil on Blood Viscosity in Peripheral Vascular Disease." *British Medical Journal* (Clinical Research) 288(1984): 592–94.

WYNDER, E. "The Dietary Environment and Cancer." *Journal of the American Dietetic Association* 71(1977): 385.

YAMORI, Y., ET AL. "Comparison of Serum Phospholipid Fatty Acids Among Fishing and Farming Japanese Populations and American Inlanders." *Journal of Nutritional Science and Vitaminology* 311(4)(1985): 417–22.

Index